PARTS OF THE GUITAR

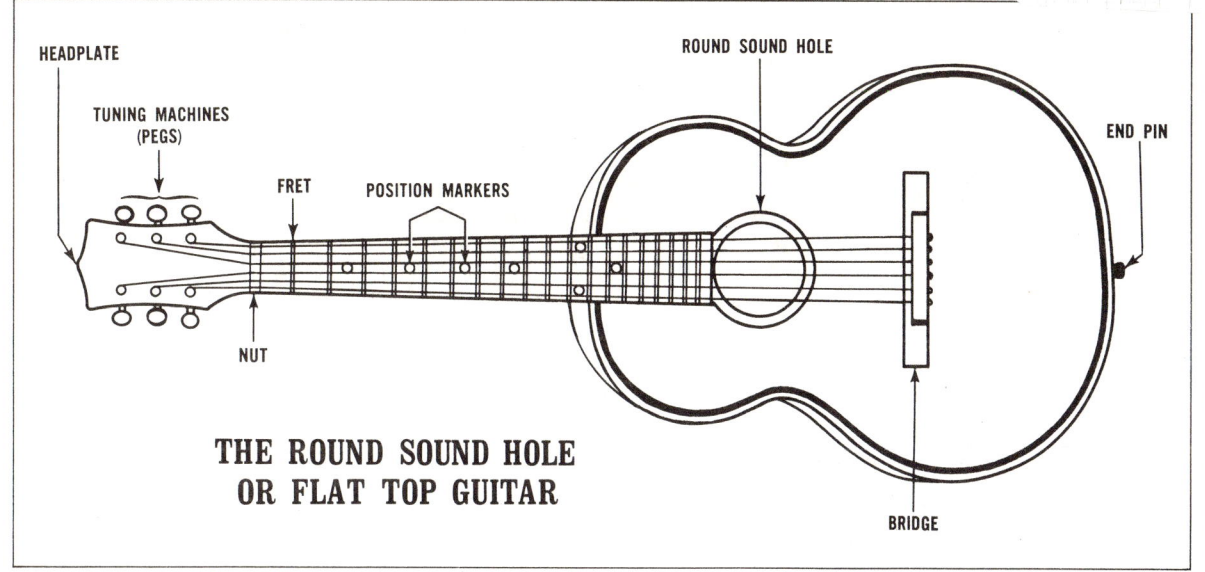

THE ROUND SOUND HOLE OR FLAT TOP GUITAR

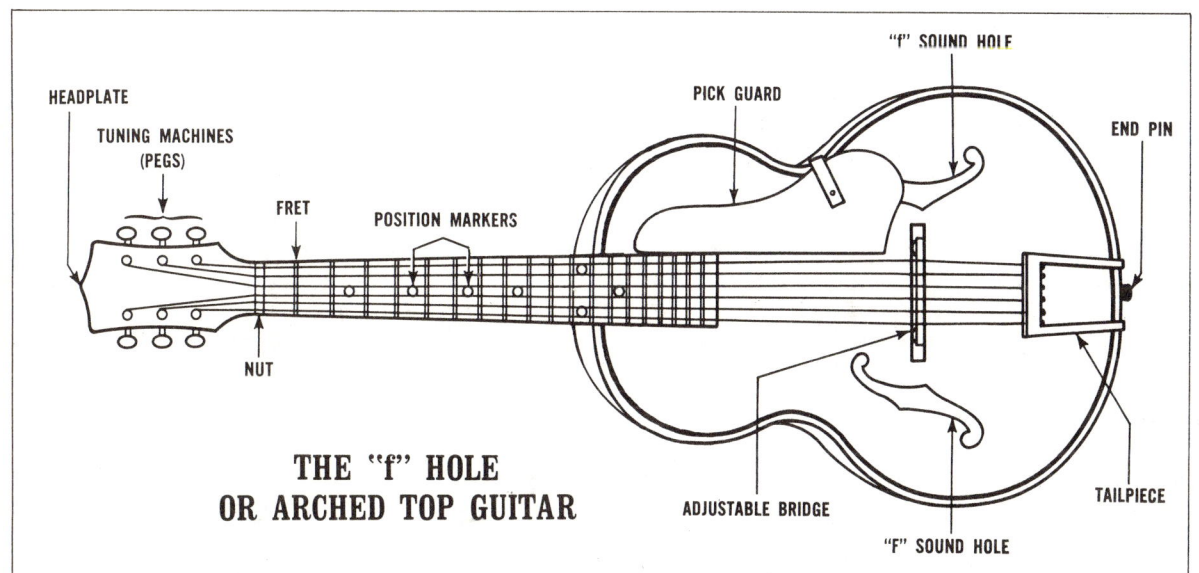

THE "f" HOLE OR ARCHED TOP GUITAR

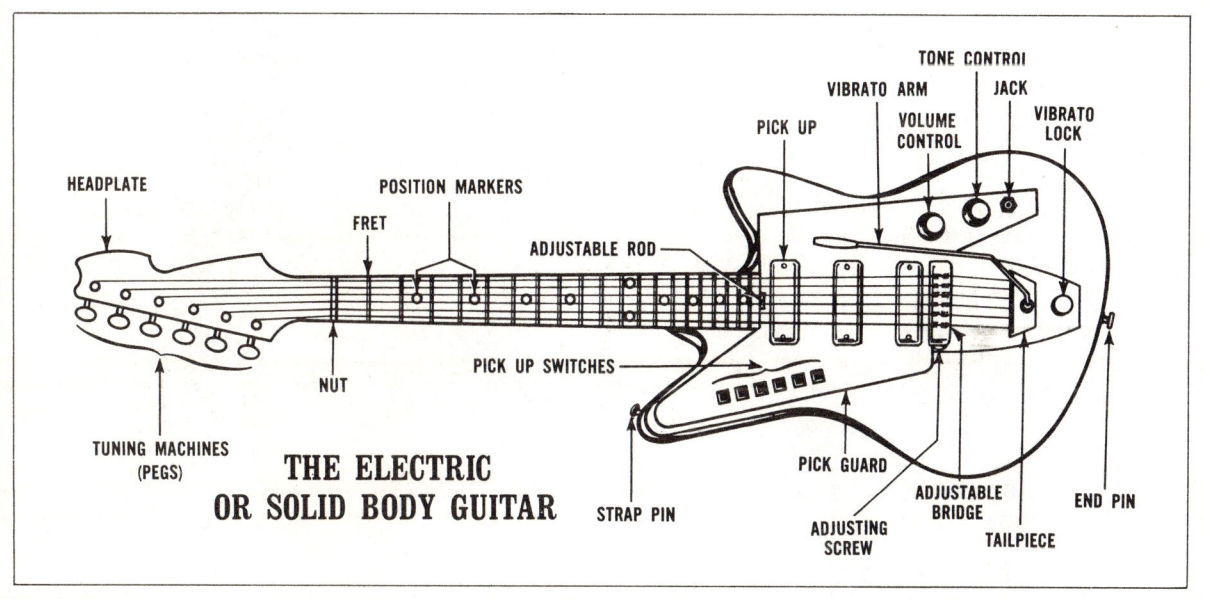

THE ELECTRIC OR SOLID BODY GUITAR

The Standard Guitar Method Book 1   © Copyright 1965 by BEACON MUSIC Co., Inc.
International copyright secured.   Made in U.S.A.

HOW TO HOLD THE GUITAR

HOW TO TUNE THE GUITAR without a pitchpipe or piano.

Tuning is a difficult procedure for the beginner. It takes a great deal of practice. If you study the guitar with a teacher, tuning will be no problem. Your teacher will guide you.

Turn pegs slowly to avoid string breakage. Make sure you turn the proper peg.

Turn the peg of the E string (the 6th, thickest string) until you get a low pitched tone (as close to the low E sound as you can remember). Then do the following:

Press 5th fret of 6th string. Pluck it
    to get pitch of 5th string (A).
Press 5th fret of 5th string. Pluck it
    to get pitch of 4th string (D).
Press 5th fret of 4th string. Pluck it
    to get pitch of 3rd string (G).
Press 4th fret of 3rd string. Pluck it
    to get pitch of 2nd string (B).
Press 5th fret of 2nd string. Pluck it
    to get pitch of 1st string (E).

You may reverse this procedure by first approximating the tone of the high E string (the 1st thin string), then going to the 5th fret of the 2nd string, etc. as shown in the diagram below.

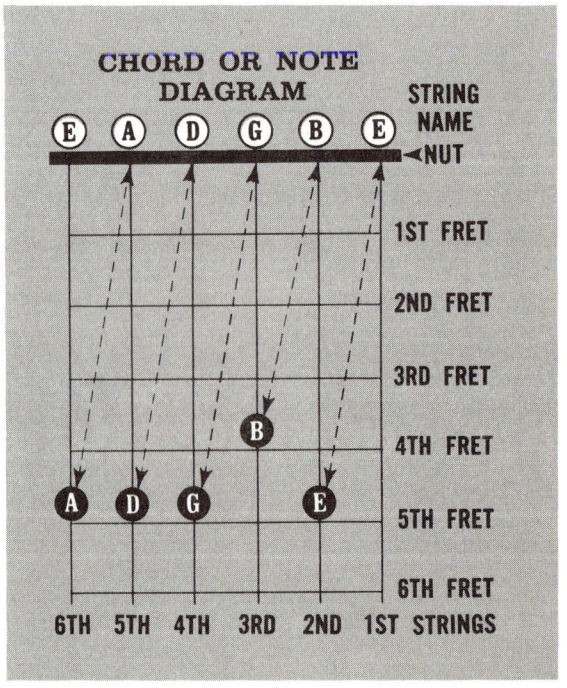

THE MUSIC STAFF

(Treble or G Clef) The staff is composed of five lines and four spaces. Lines and spaces are always counted from the bottom.

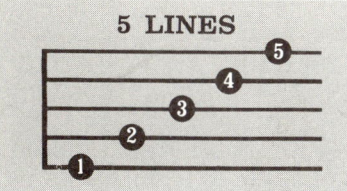
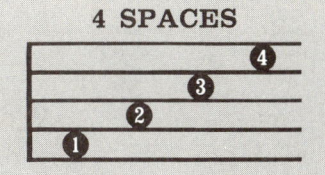

Lines and spaces can be referred to by number or by letter name. The first seven letters of the alphabet are used to name the notes, thus we have A, B, C, D, E, F, G, repeated many..times..depending on the musical range needed to write a composition. The alphabet will occur on alternate lines and spaces in the staff.

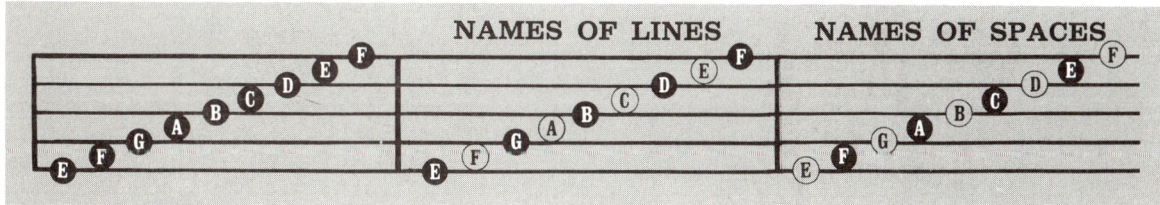

Leger Lines

The staff can be extended by additional lines added above or below.

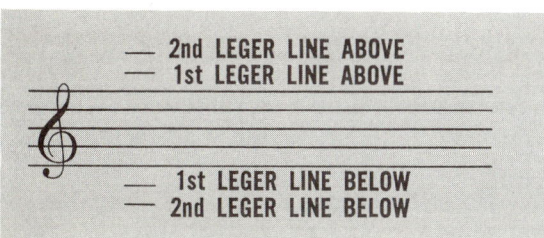

Measures

Music is divided into measures. Bar lines separate each measure.

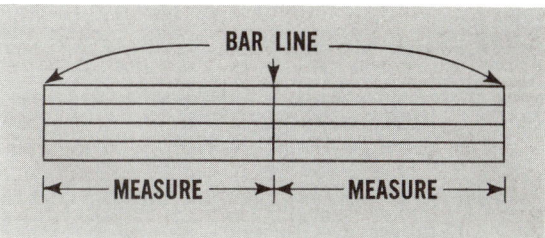

Time Signature

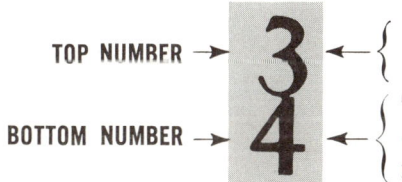

TOP NUMBER → 3 { Tells the number of counts in a measure.

BOTTOM NUMBER → 4 { Tells what kind of note receives one count. In this case a quarter note receives one count.

Notes are signs by which music is written on paper.
The style of the note indicates the time value.

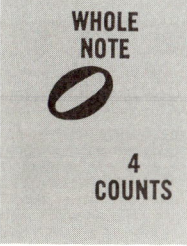
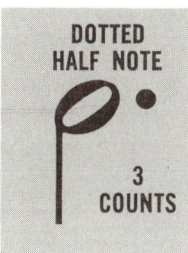
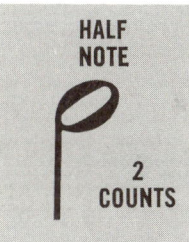

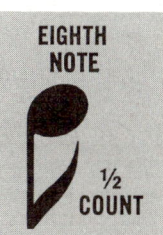

TECHNIQUE

LEFT HAND

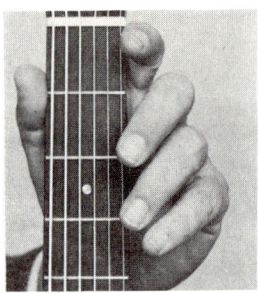

POSITION WHEN PLAYING OPEN STRINGS (Fingers curled and poised to drop on strings.)

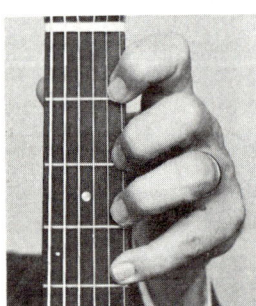

POSITION WHEN FINGERING (Fingers curled, using tips. Wrist extremely bent.)

A proper left hand position is essential. Fingers should be curled and only the fingertips should be placed on the string.

The fingers should be placed on the strings precisely and with decision. Too much pressure will result in undue fatigue and cause a cramped hand position.

As the fingertips harden they will strike the strings with a hammering effect. This action, combined with the proper timing of the pick, will produce the best tone with the least effort.

The desired pitch is obtained by pressing (or stopping) the string against a fret. Play as close to the fret as possible. The proper position is right behind the fret . . . never on it.

The left hand nails must be kept short enough to allow the fingertip to press the string against the fingerboard without interference.

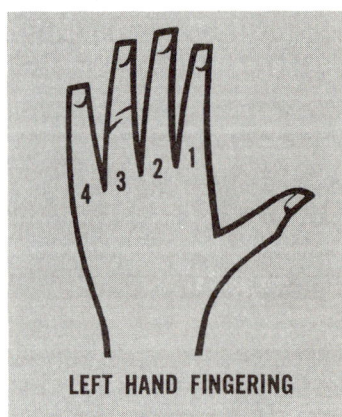

LEFT HAND FINGERING

O MEANS "OPEN"

RIGHT HAND

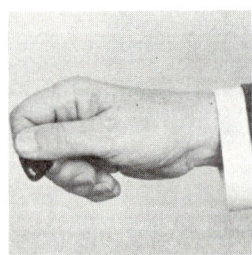 

SINGLE STRING (PICKING)

The pick should be held in a loose and relaxed grip. Do not stiffen fingers in a straight position. It will be helpful to allow several fingers to glide across the top of the guitar (or guard plate) in order to maintain a level stroke with the pick. Use very short pick strokes, keeping the pick close to the strings after playing each note. This will avoid the need for looking at the strings before playing another note.

The guitar should be picked softly to produce the best possible tone. Allow the string to vibrate freely. Do not touch the vibrating string with the pick before it is time for the next note.

CHORDS (STRUMMING)

Single notes are picked.
Chords are strummed.

A chord is a group of three or more notes . . . on different strings . . . played at the same time.

The right hand movement, while strumming chords, will vary according to the number of strings you wish to play. Do **not** try to rest, or brace your hand against the guitar top. Try to achieve a loose, relaxed stroke. Slant the pick slightly to allow it to glide across the strings. Strum slowly and softly until the best possible tone is produced.

OPEN STRINGS (Not stopped by a finger)

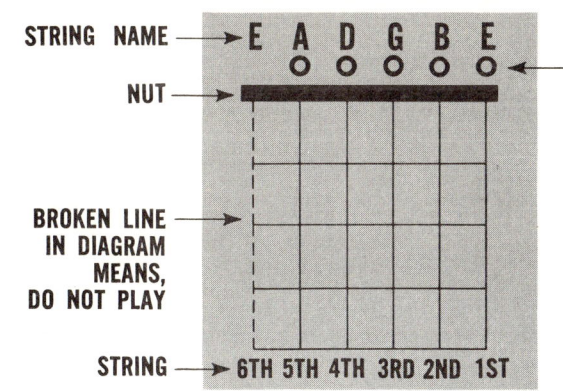

RIGHT HAND PLAYING POSITION

EXERCISE USING THE FIRST THREE OPEN STRINGS (E--B--G)

1. Place the right hand in the proper playing position as shown in photo above. The left hand will not be used during this exercise. All of these notes should be played by picking downward. The use of the upward stroke will be explained later. The down pick is shown thus: ⊓

2. Pick the first (E) string several times to establish the pitch in your mind. Make very short strokes with the pick. This will keep the pick so close to the string there will be no need to watch it.

3. With your hand in the same position, a slight reach will enable you to pick the second (B) string. This will sound lower than the first string. Pick the B string several times, and then pick the E string several times. You can quickly recognize the difference.

4. Pick open E several times... then open B several times. Reach a little further and pick the third (G) string. This will be the lowest of the three strings. Pick each string several times until you can recognize their sound without looking at them.

5. Pick E, B, E, B, then E and B together. Pick B, G, B, G, then B and G together. Play various combinations of these three strings until you can select any string, or strings, without glancing at them.

NOW PLAY THIS

© Copyright 1965 by BEACON MUSIC Co., Inc.
International copyright secured.   Made in U.S.A.

THREE NOTES ON THE E OR 1ST STRING

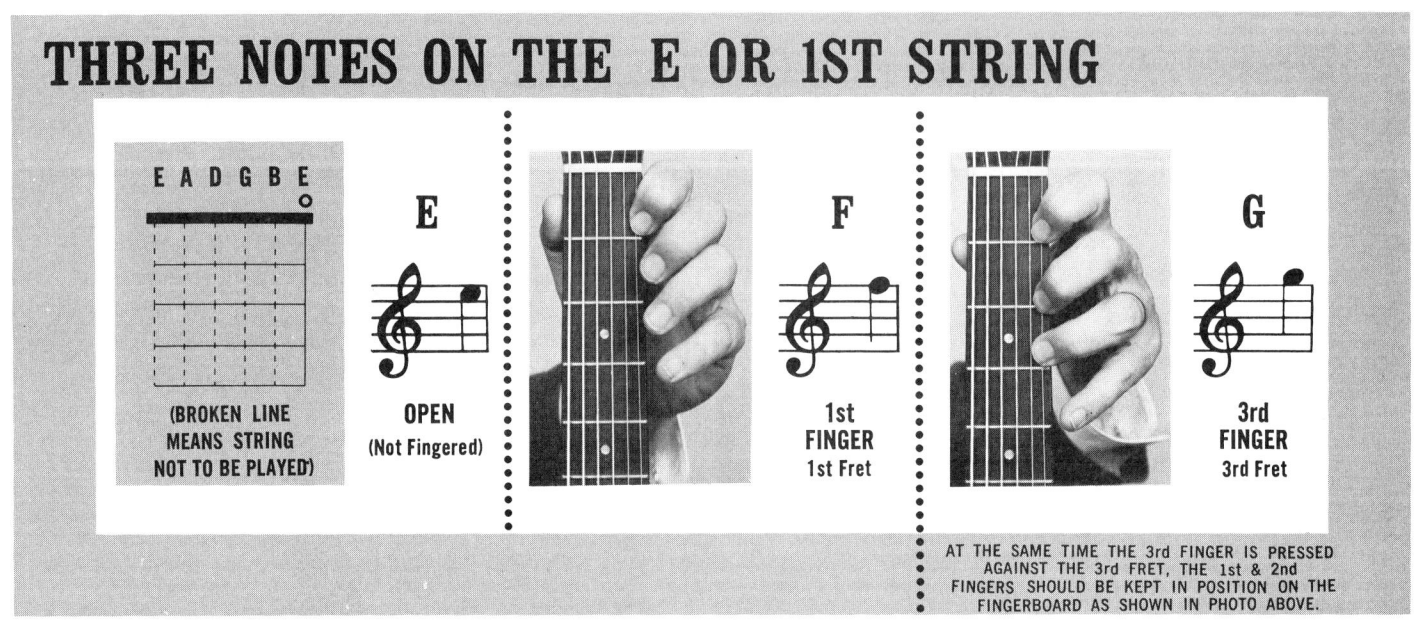

USE DOWN STROKES FOR ALL NOTES.

TWO NOTES   E (open)   F (1st finger)

THREE NOTES   E (open)   F (1st finger)   G (Third finger)

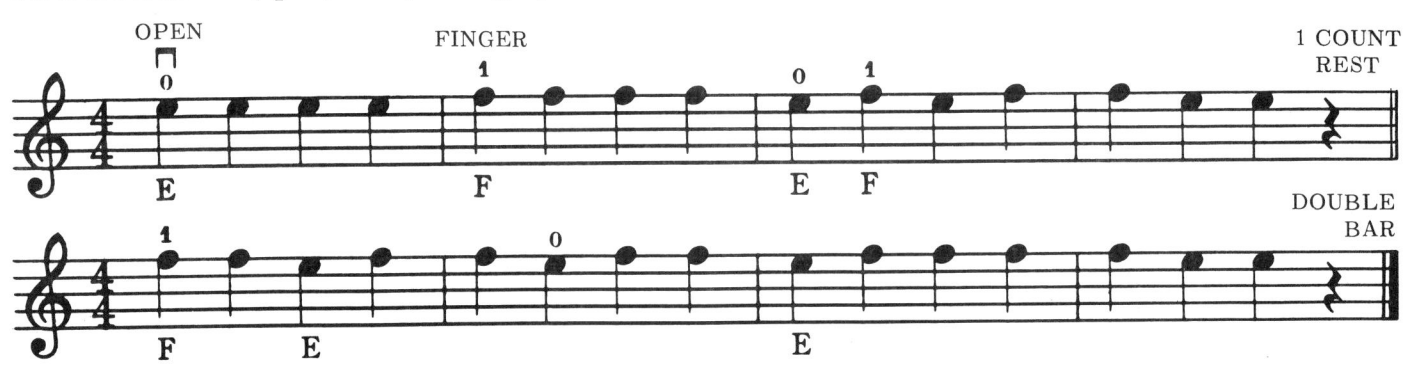

PLAYING E, F, G, WITH MELODIC SKIPS

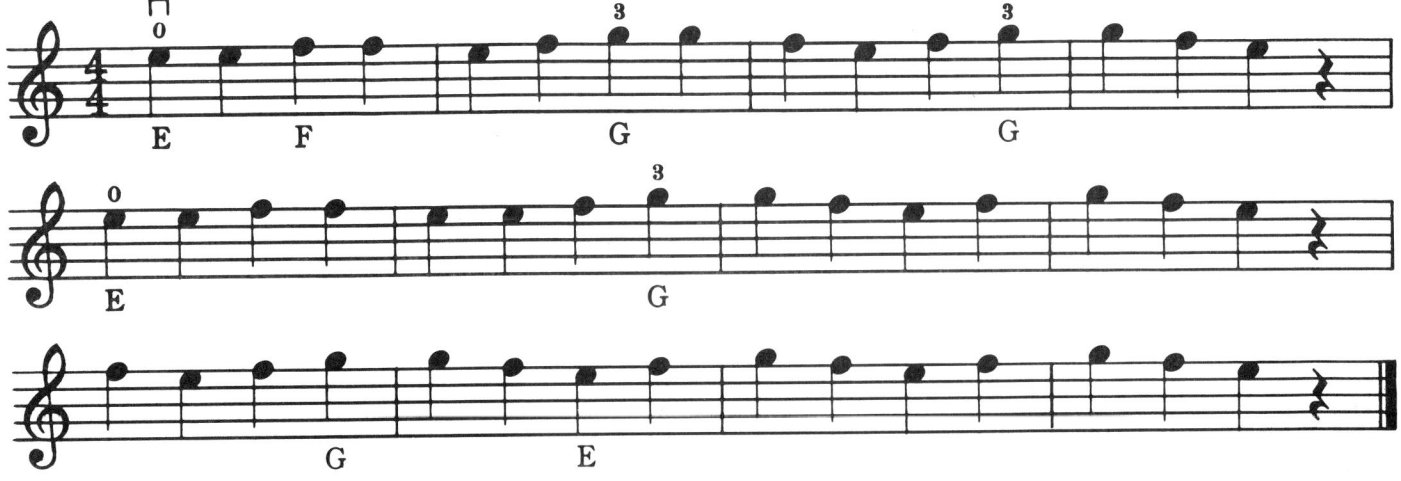

INTRODUCING HALF NOTES

 Every half note must be held for two full counts. Keep finger in position. Allow the note to ring. Do not blur the tone by setting the pick against the vibrating string in preparation for the next note. COUNT ALOUD while LEARNING THIS SONG. Count ONE when the note is picked and count TWO while it is being held.

tick tock

an easy waltz

A dotted half note (d·) must be held for three full counts. Count ONE when it is picked and count TWO, THREE while holding the note.

THREE NOTES ON THE B OR 2ND STRING

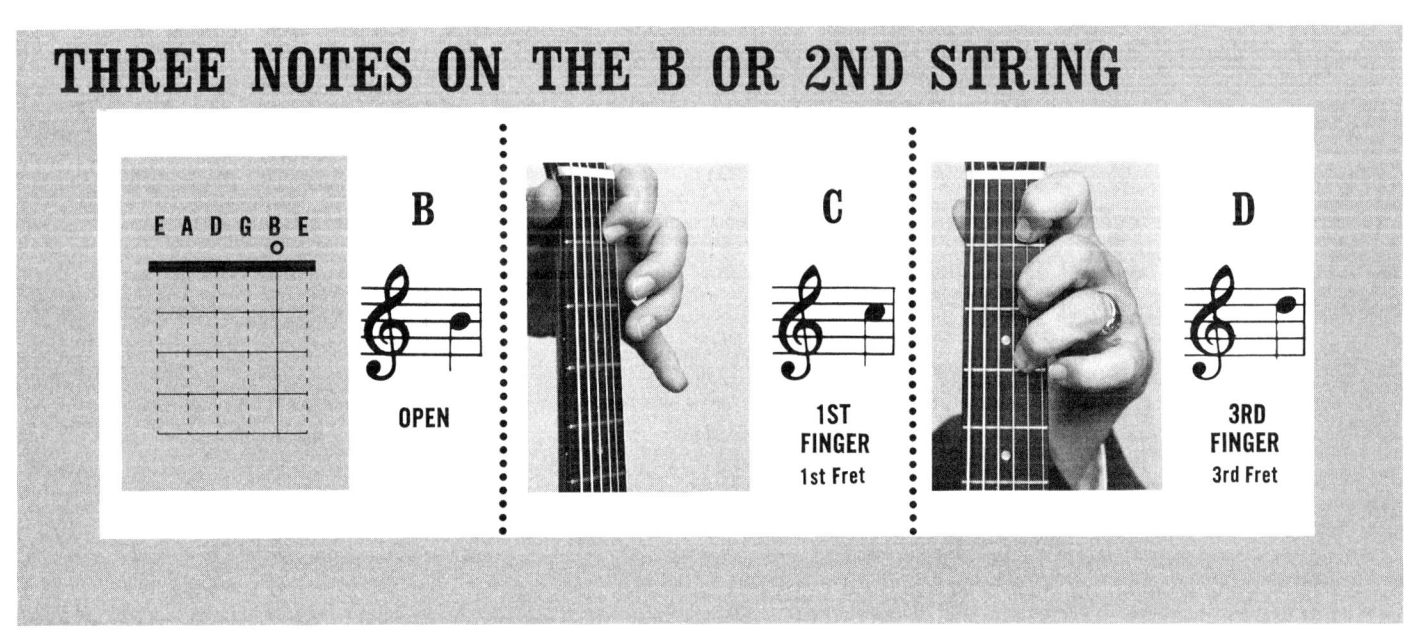

TWO NOTES   B (open)   C (1st finger)

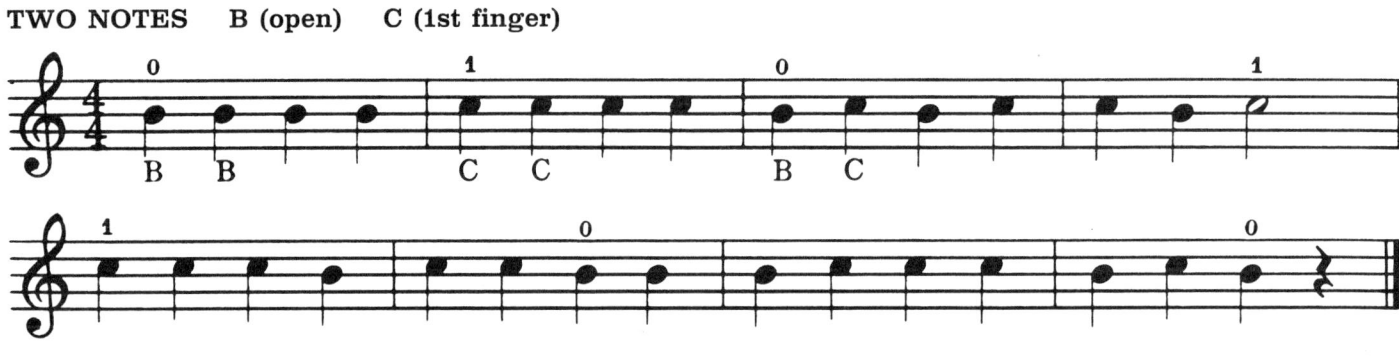

THREE NOTES   B (open)   C (1st finger)   D (3rd finger)

THREE NOTES WITH MELODIC SKIPS

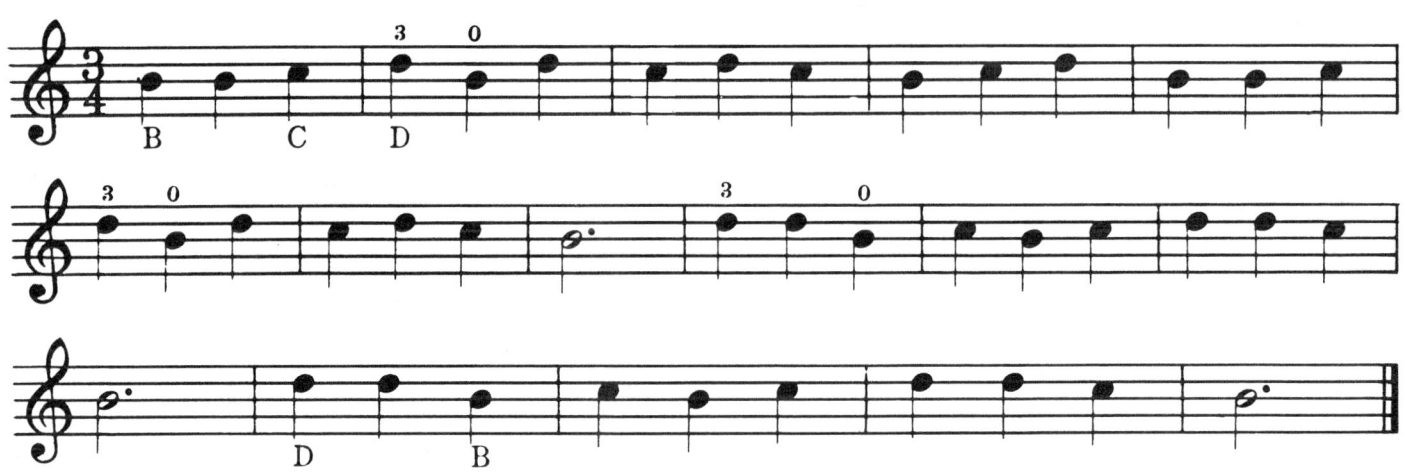

READING NOTES ON TWO STRINGS

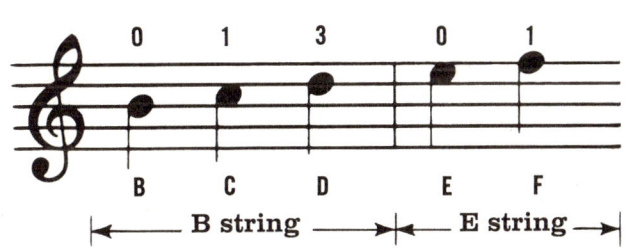

countdown

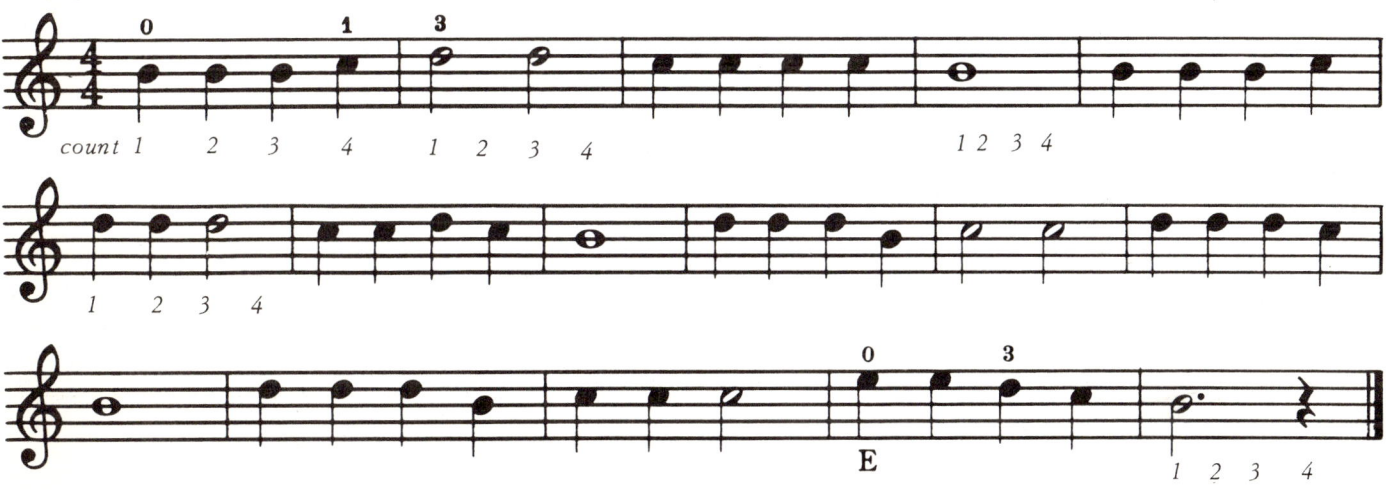

yankee doodle

barbara ann waltz

NOTES ON THE E & B STRING

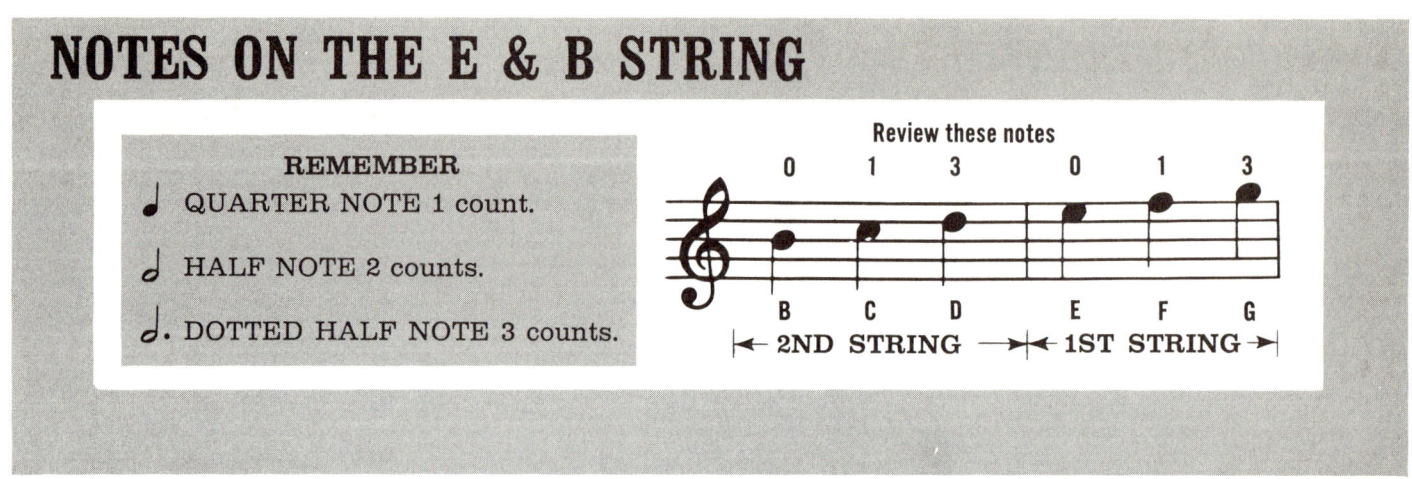

jingle bells (SIMPLIFIED) 5 DIFFERENT NOTES

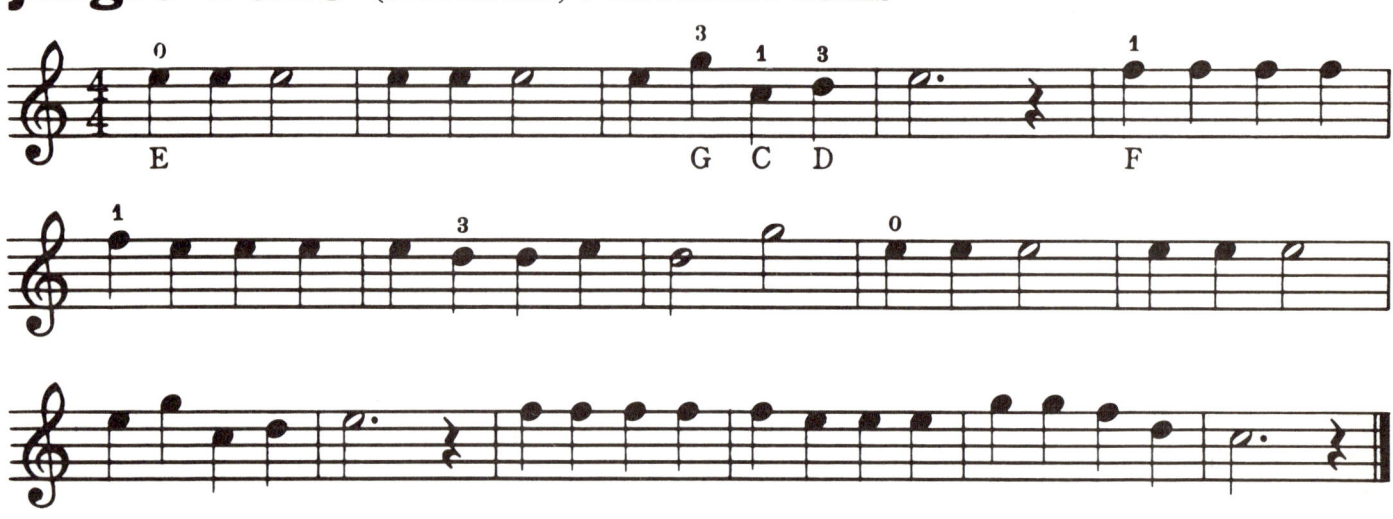

choral 6 DIFFERENT NOTES

Not fast — Beethoven (modified)

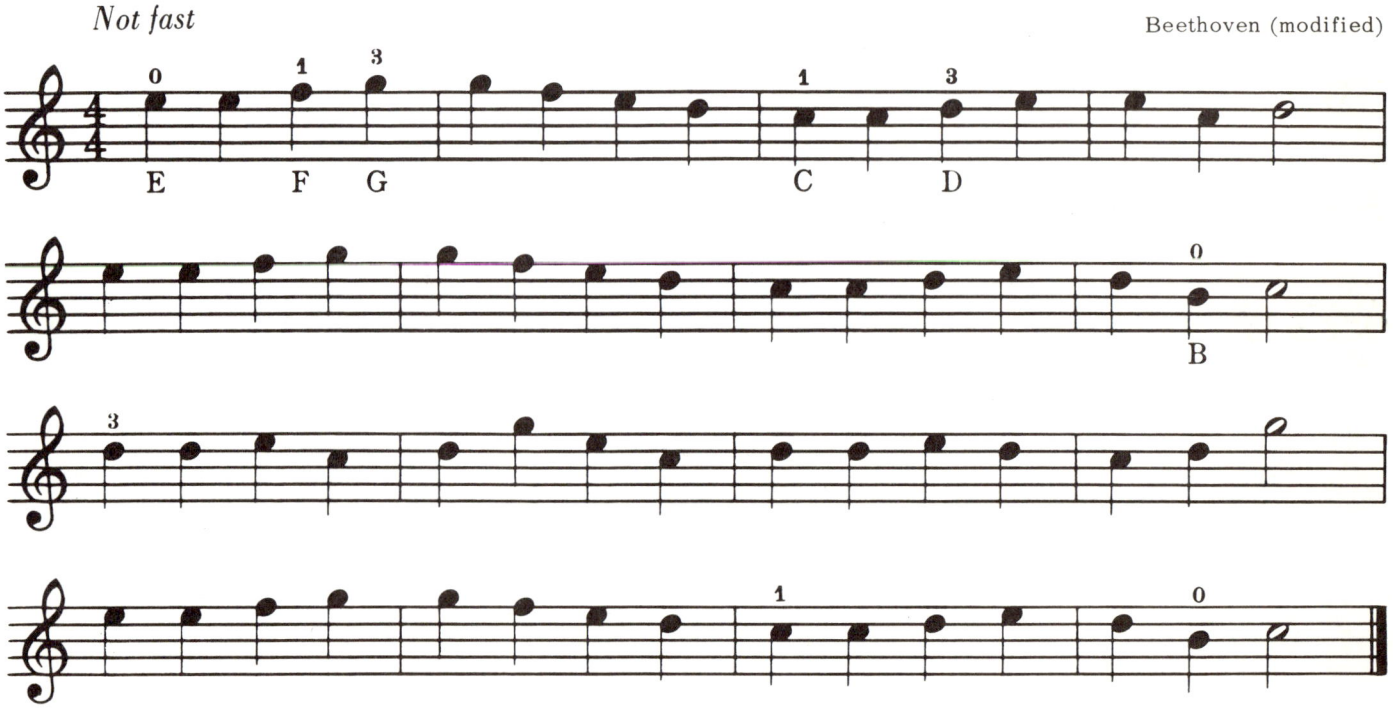

SIMPLIFIED CHORDS IN DIAGRAM FORM

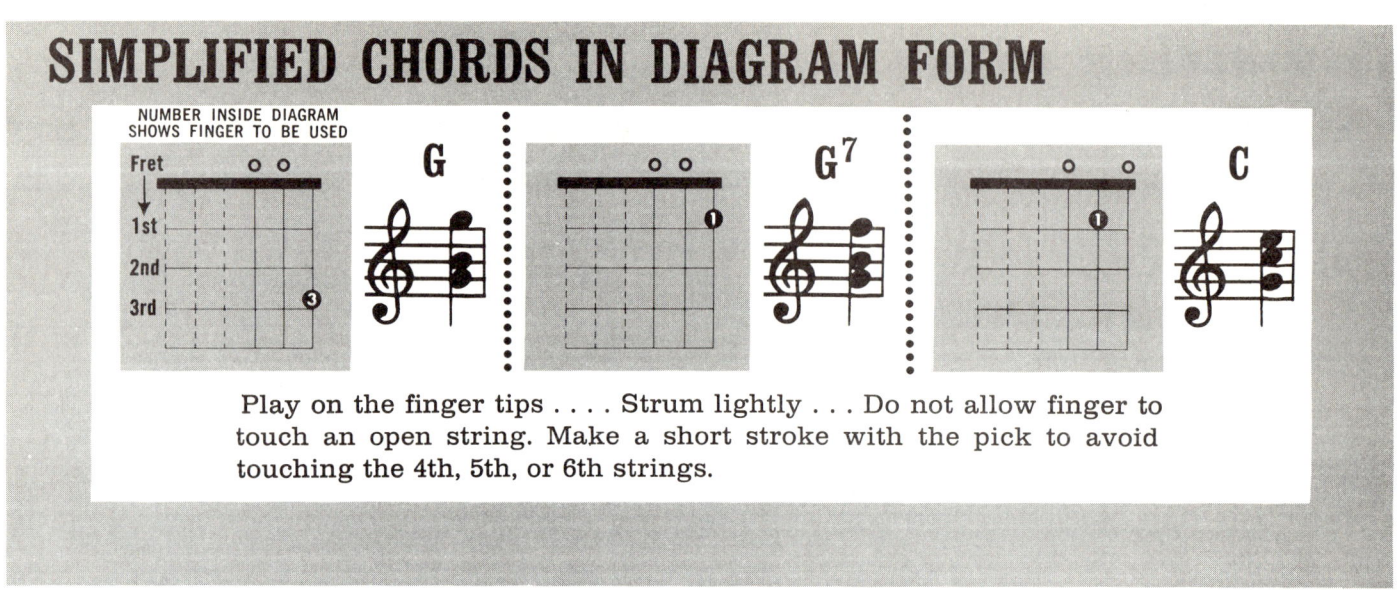

Play on the finger tips .... Strum lightly ... Do not allow finger to touch an open string. Make a short stroke with the pick to avoid touching the 4th, 5th, or 6th strings.

simplified chords in musical notation

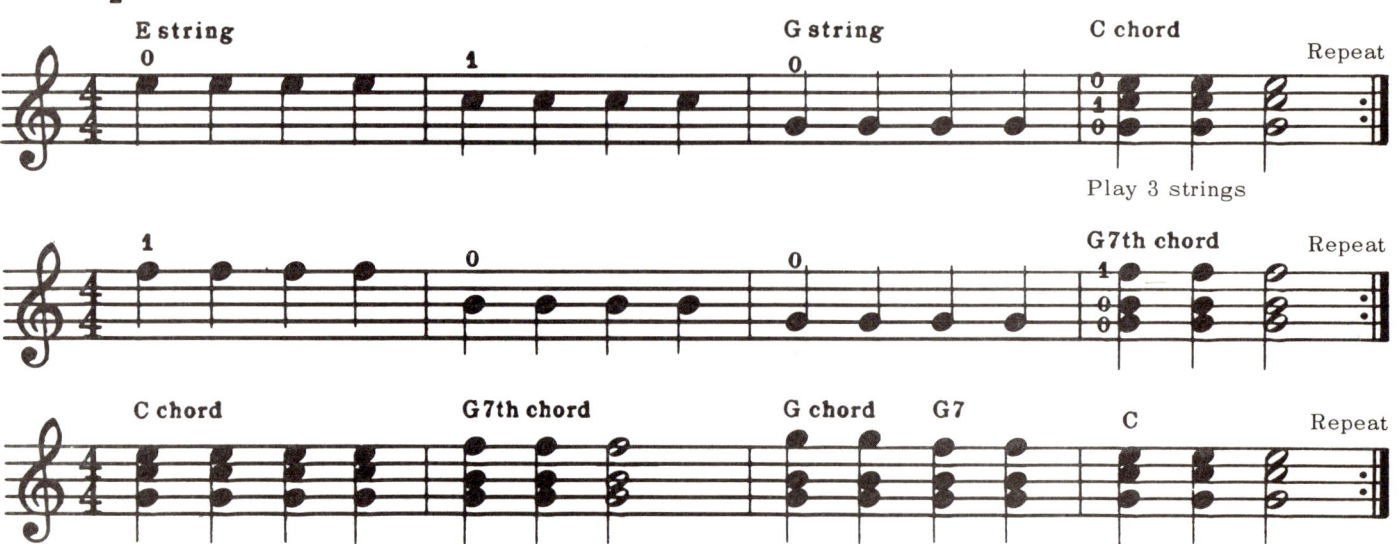

melody and chords
Practice slowly ... Do not hurry the single notes ... Do not delay the chords.

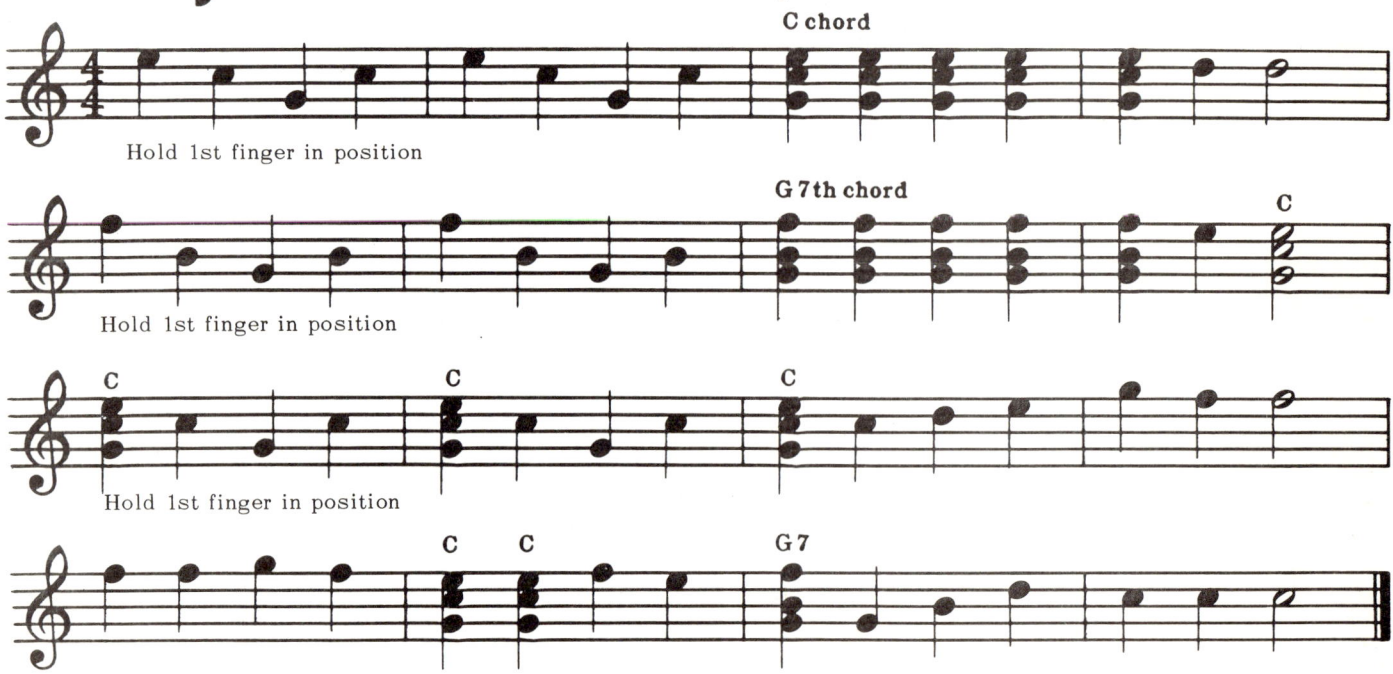

Accolade

Music for two guitars is arranged by joining two staffs with an ACCOLADE, also called a BRACE.

One guitar may play the upper line while another guitar plays the lower line. Also, the lower line may be used to accompany a voice.

Double bar

Double bars are used as points of division in a musical arrangement. The light double bar indicates the end of a certain portion of the piece. The heavy double bar indicates the final ending.

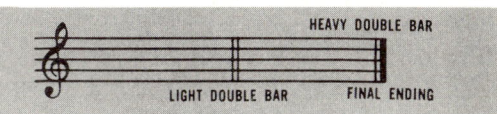

Simplified Chord Notation

The same chord repeated many times may be shown by a series of diagonal lines, //. Each line indicates a chord. The following line of music will illustrate. The 1st and 2nd measures are played the same way. The 3rd and 4th measures should be played like the 5th and 6th measures.

down in the valley

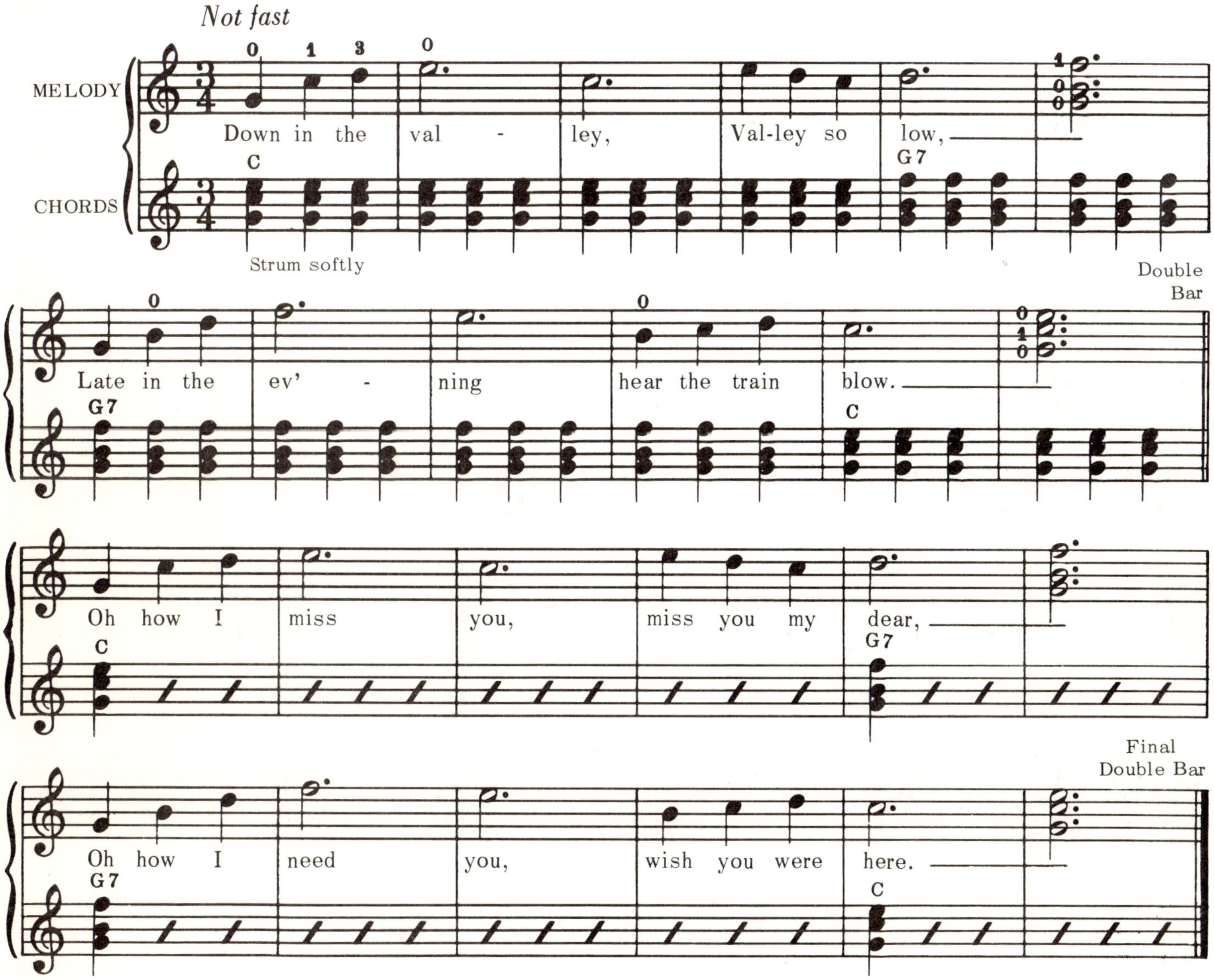

Not fast

MELODY / CHORDS

Down in the val - ley, Val-ley so low,
C   G7
Strum softly
                                          Double Bar

Late in the ev' - ning hear the train blow.
G7   C

Oh how I miss you, miss you my dear,
C   G7
                                          Final Double Bar

Oh how I need you, wish you were here.
G7   C

13

NOTE ON THE G OR 3RD STRING

A

2nd Finger
2nd Fret

As the student approaches the lower strings there will be a tendency to flatten the finger to aid in reaching across the fingerboard. This should be avoided by arching the wrist and playing on the fingertips.

lightly row
MIXING NOTES ON THE B AND G STRINGS

two string waltz

swingin' an' pickin' (melody and chords)

1st finger can remain in position . . . .

1st finger can remain in position . . . .

twinkle, twinkle, little star

elva lee waltz

EIGHTH NOTES

BODY STEM FLAG EIGHTH NOTE

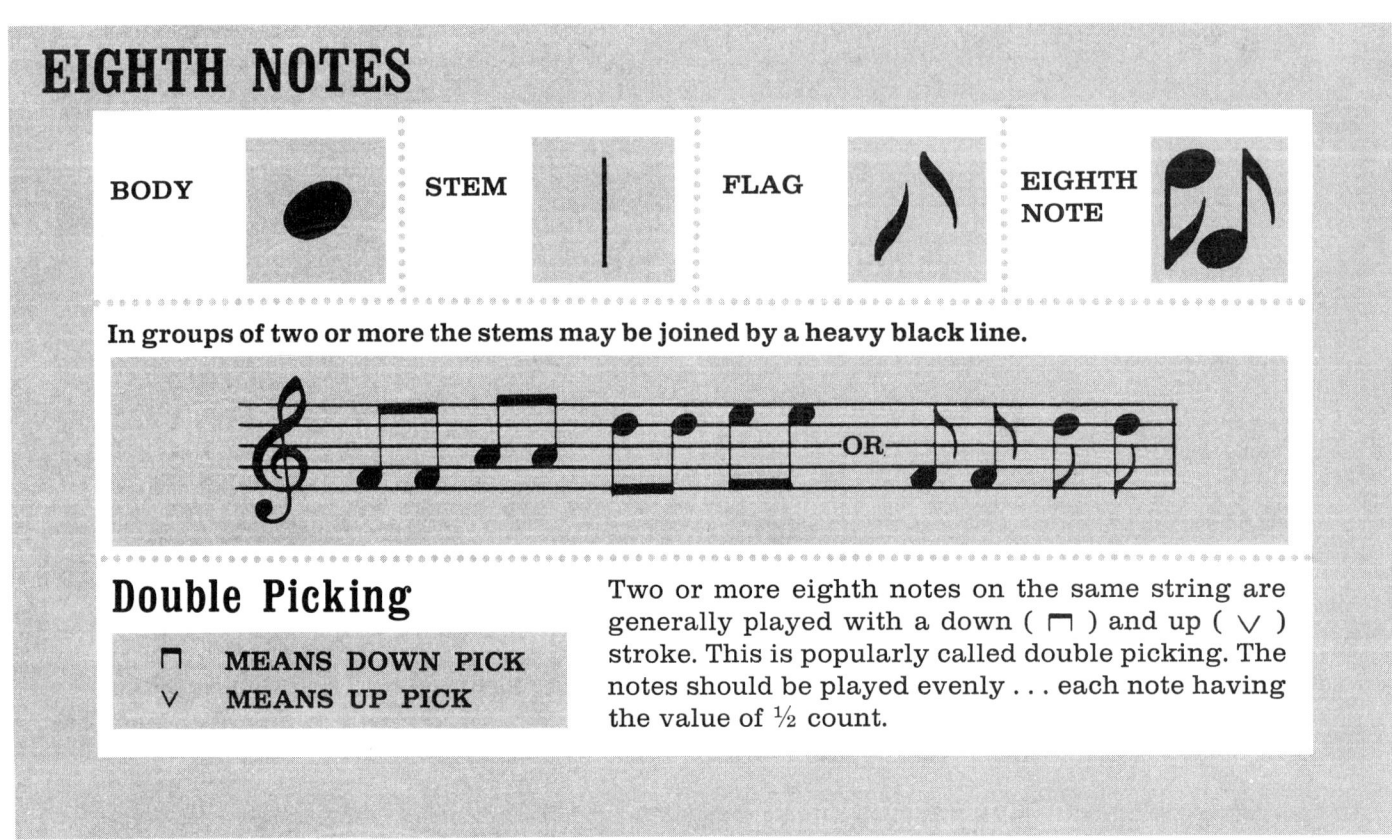

In groups of two or more the stems may be joined by a heavy black line.

OR

Double Picking

⊓ MEANS DOWN PICK
V MEANS UP PICK

Two or more eighth notes on the same string are generally played with a down (⊓) and up (V) stroke. This is popularly called double picking. The notes should be played evenly . . . each note having the value of ½ count.

EIGHTH NOTES PLAYED ON THE 1ST COUNT IN A MEASURE

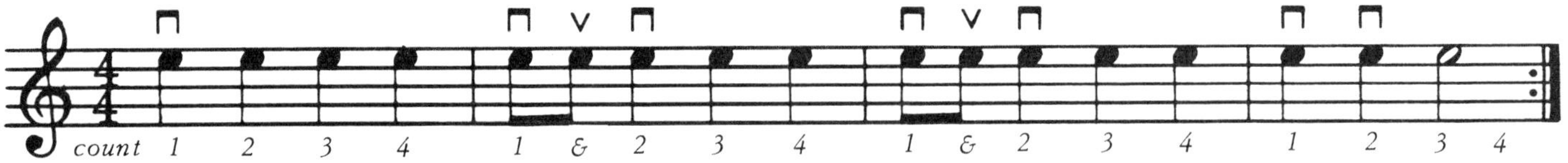

count 1 2 3 4 1 & 2 3 4 1 & 2 3 4 1 2 3 4

EIGHTH NOTES ON THE SECOND COUNT

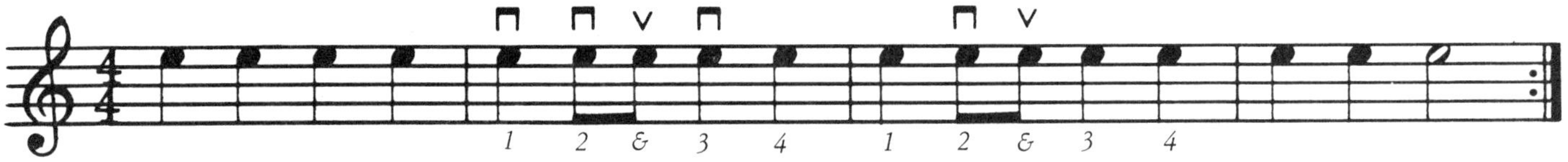

1 2 & 3 4 1 2 & 3 4

EIGHTH NOTES ON THE THIRD COUNT

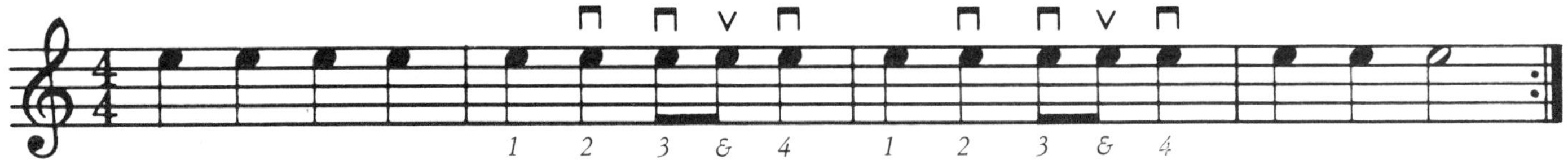

1 2 3 & 4 1 2 3 & 4

EIGHTH NOTES ON THE FOURTH COUNT

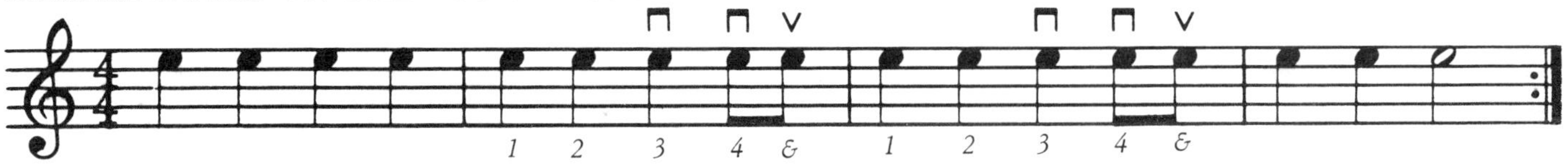

1 2 3 4 & 1 2 3 4 &

4 EIGHTH NOTES IN ONE MEASURE

1 2 3 & 4 1 & 2 & 3 4 1 2 & 3 4

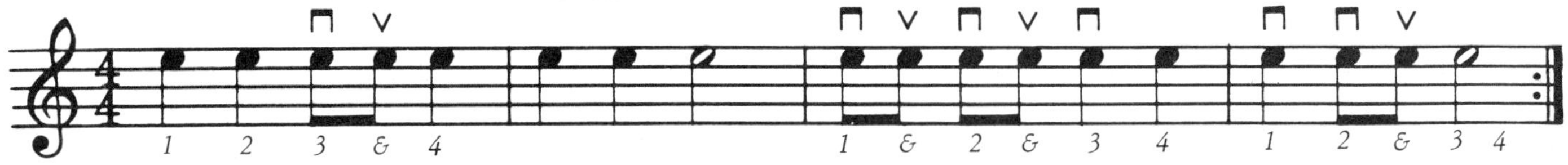

8 EIGHTH NOTES IN ONE MEASURE

1 & 2 3 4 1 2 3 & 4 & 1 & 2 & 3 & 4 & 1 2 & 3 4

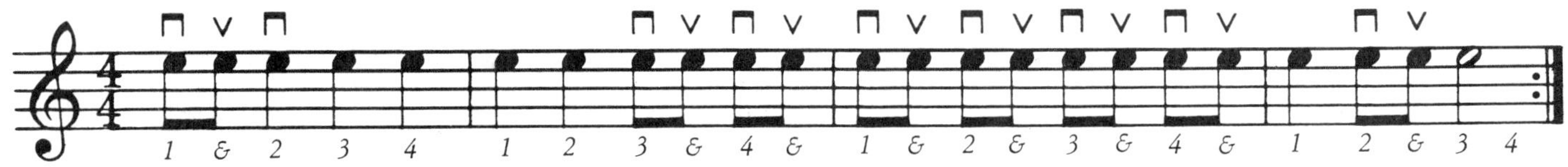

DA CAPO	To the beginning / To the top / To the head	Abbreviated **D. C. al Fine**
al FINE	Finish / End	D. C. al Fine means; Return to the beginning of the selection and play to Fine.

tom dooley

Hang down your head Tom Doo-ley, Hang down your head and cry,

Hang down your head Tom Doo-ley, Poor boy you're gon-na die. *Fine*

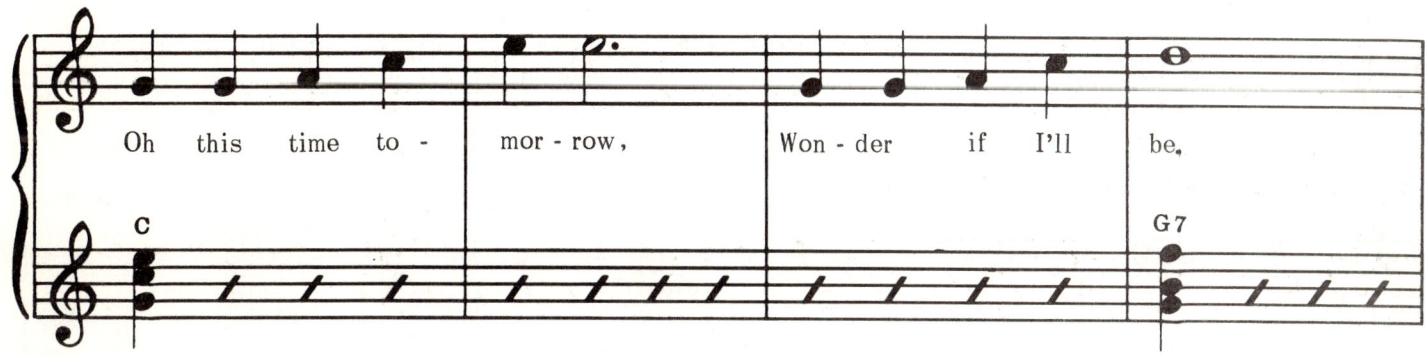
Oh this time to-mor-row, Won-der if I'll be,

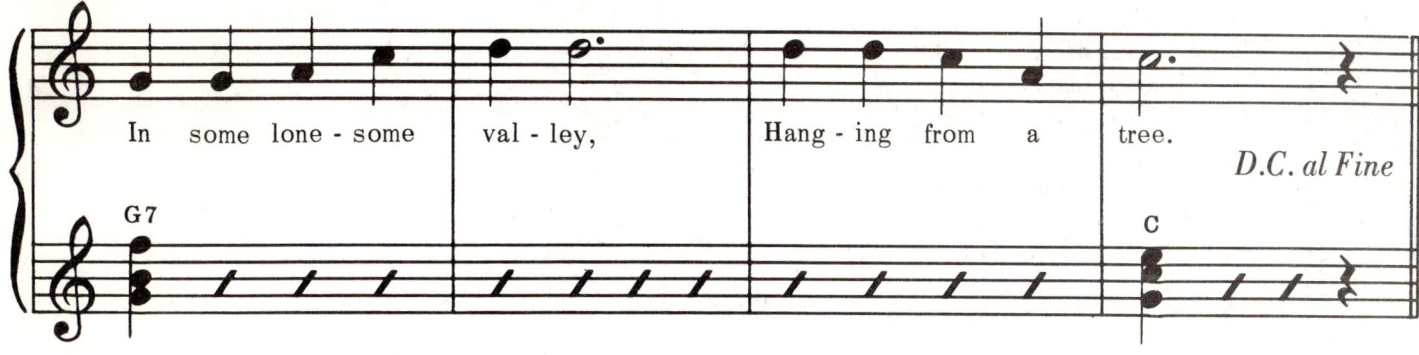
In some lone-some val-ley, Hang-ing from a tree. *D.C. al Fine*

HOW TO PRACTICE

PRACTICE MEANS: To perform or work at repeatedly; to acquire skill or proficiency.

The old adage "Practice Makes Perfect" does not hold true unless the practice time is applied to learn a piece correctly.

Any difficult measure or group of notes that presents a problem should be practiced separately. Drill on that particular problem until it is mastered. Some of the measures in Skip To My Lou are shown as examples.

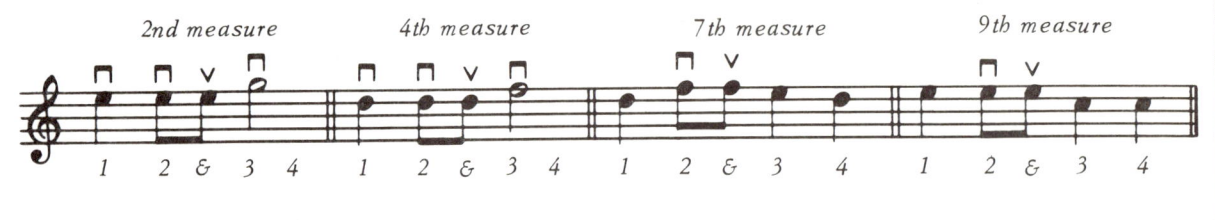

skip to my lou (SQUARE DANCE)

Sharp – raises the pitch of a note by one half-step, one half-tone, one fret on the guitar.

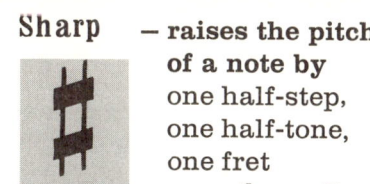

Flat – lowers the pitch of a note by one half-step, one half-tone, one fret on the guitar.

Natural – cancels a previous sharp or flat and restores a note to its usual pitch.

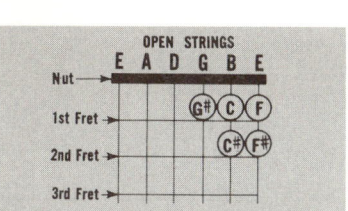

Time Signature

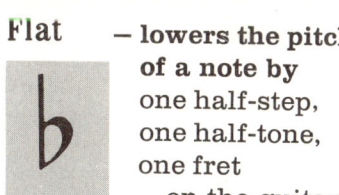

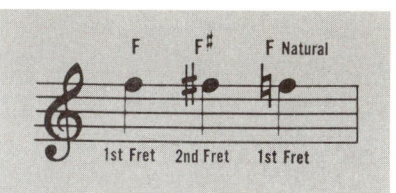

Key Signature

The sharp on the 5th line (F) indicates the key of G. In this key all F's will be raised to F♯ (1 fret higher).

Key and Time Signature

Always study the key and the time signature before playing a song.

Use of Natural Sign in Key of G

The natural sign (♮) may be used to cancel the F♯ in a particular measure or a part of a measure.

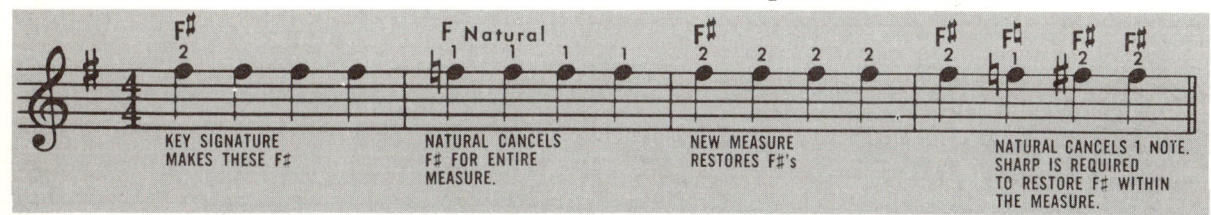

KEY SIGNATURE MAKES THESE F♯. NATURAL CANCELS F♯ FOR ENTIRE MEASURE. NEW MEASURE RESTORES F♯'s. NATURAL CANCELS 1 NOTE. SHARP IS REQUIRED TO RESTORE F♯ WITHIN THE MEASURE.

SCALE OF G

(SHOULD BE MEMORIZED) The scale of G begins on G and ends on G. In this scale we use F♯ instead of the usual F. Other notes will be in usual position.

SCALE OF G USING VARIOUS RHYTHMS

THE D7th CHORD

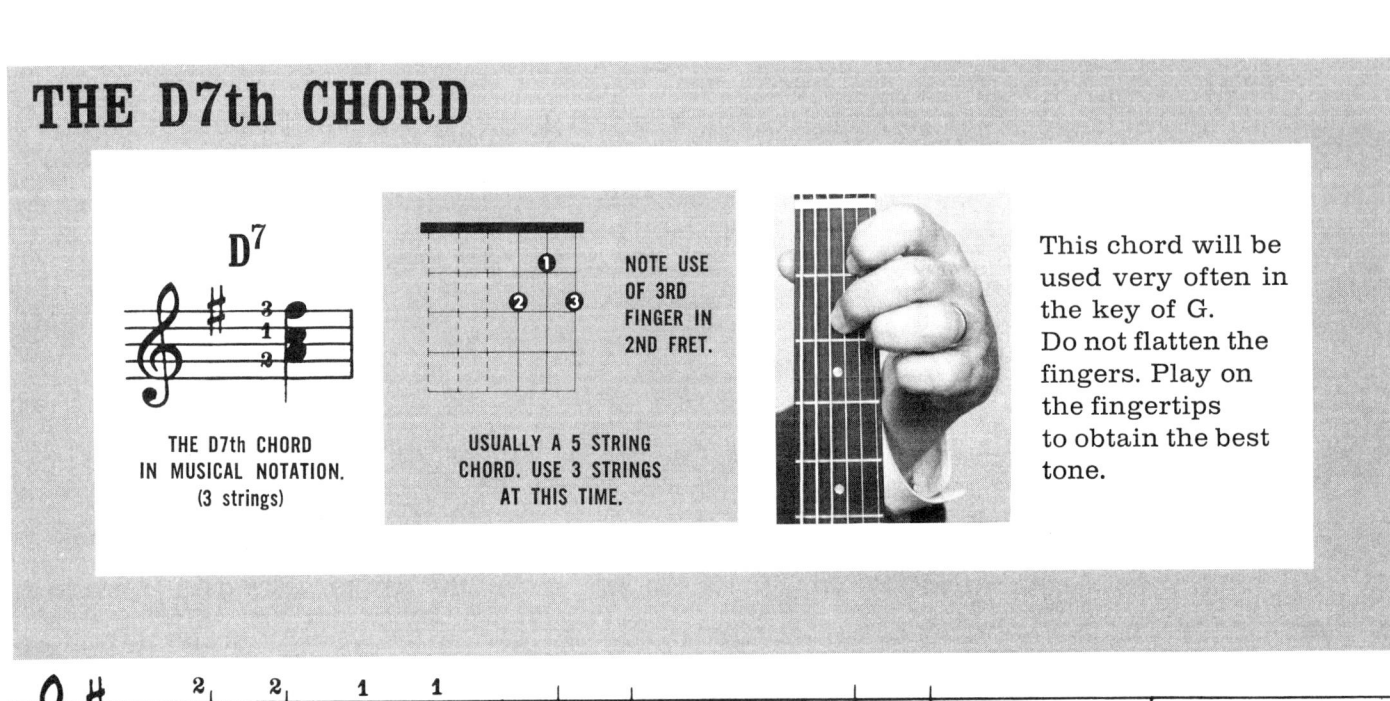

Keep 1st finger in position ....

Keep 2nd finger in position ....

beautiful brown eyes

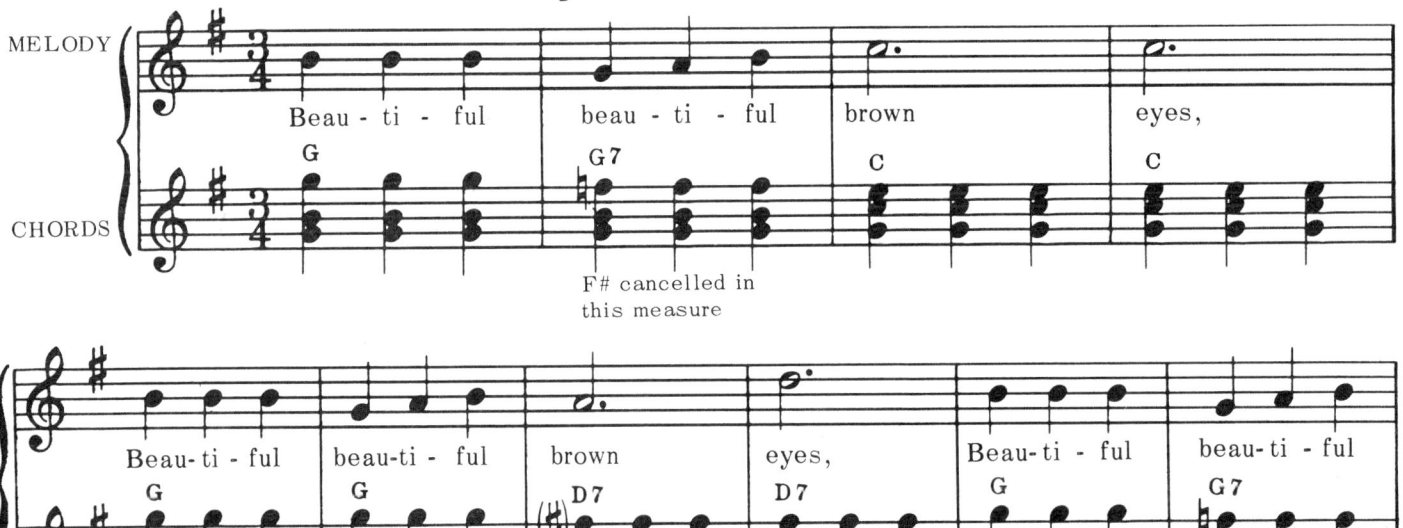

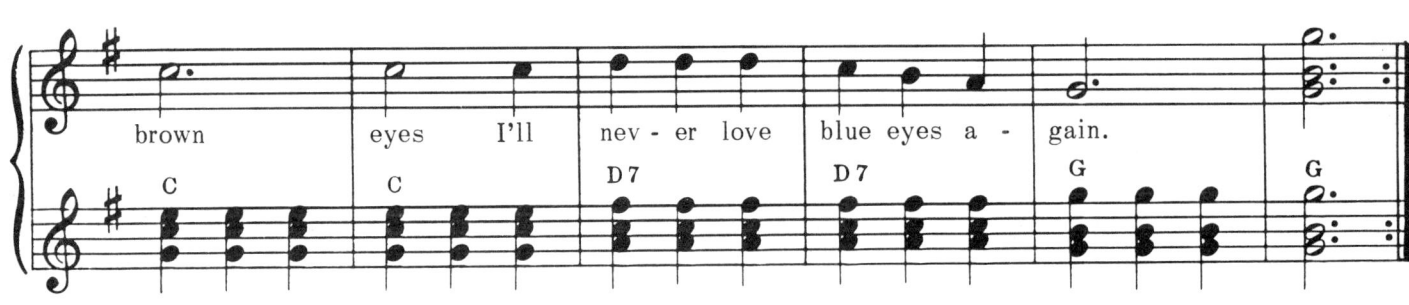

INCOMPLETE MEASURES (explanation and examples)

The top number of the time signature indicates the number of counts in each full measure of a composition.

The first and last measures may not be complete, but the total count will make a full measure.

When the first measure does not contain the number of counts shown in the time signature, the remaining counts will be found in the final measure.

ACCIDENTALS are flats or sharps that occur in a piece but are not a part of the key signature. They only affect the measure in which they are placed.

tisket, a tasket

This song begins with an incomplete measure. (1 count) The two dots and double bar at the end of the 3rd line means, "Repeat the entire selection." Do not delay when repeating. The 3 counts in the last measure plus the 1 count in the 1st measure will make 4 counts.

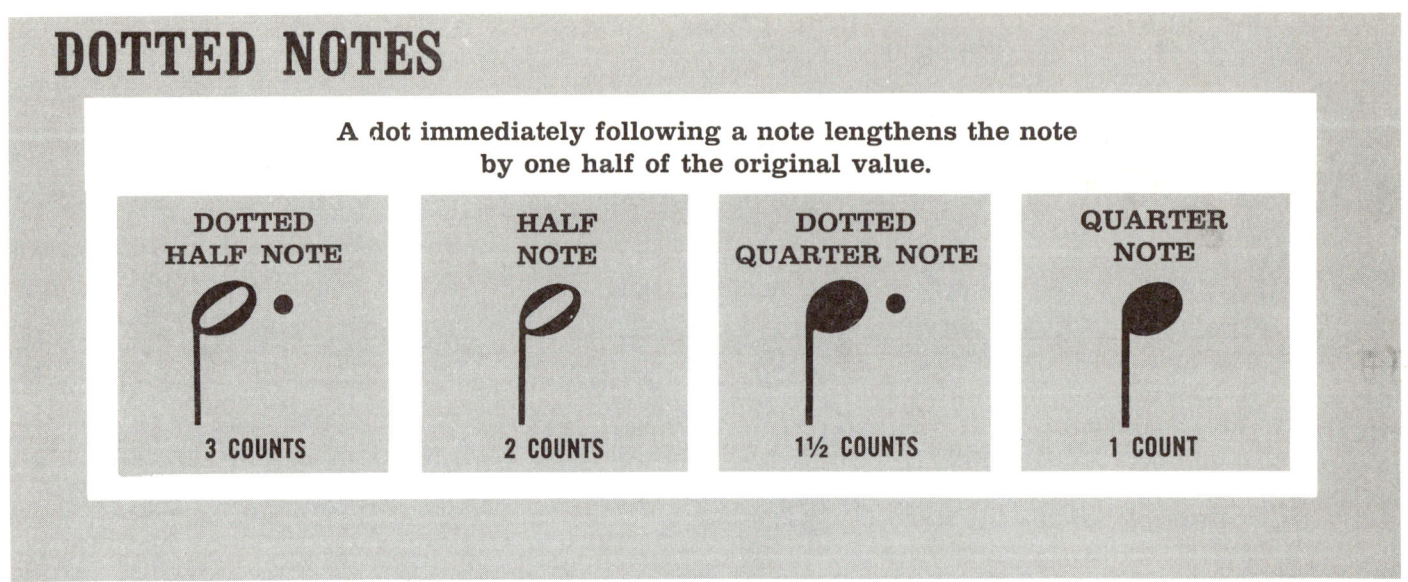

counting dotted notes

streets of laredo

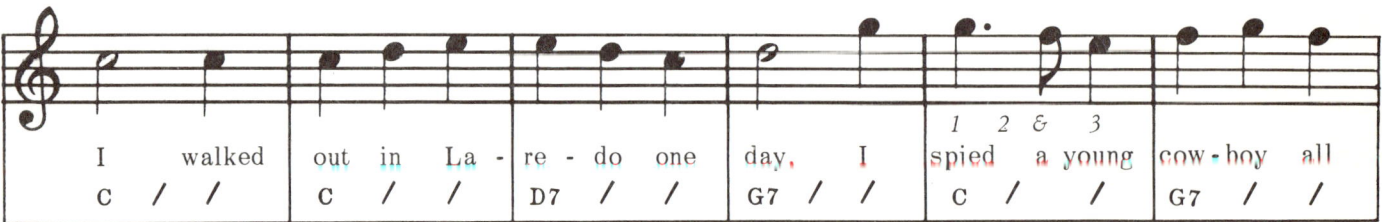
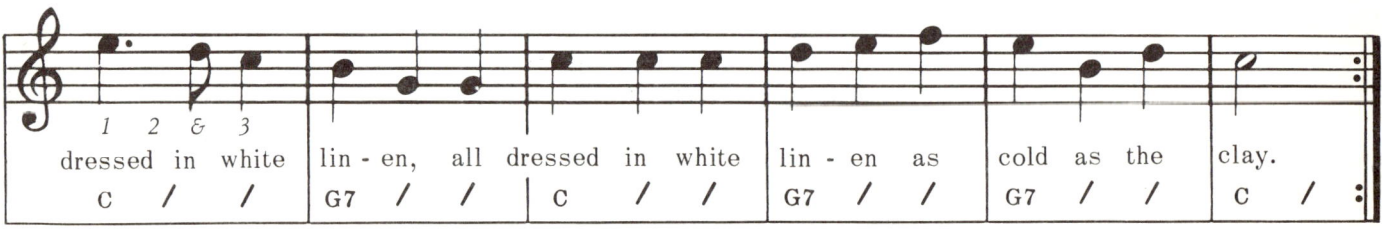

FORMING 4 STRING CHORDS BY ADDING OPEN D

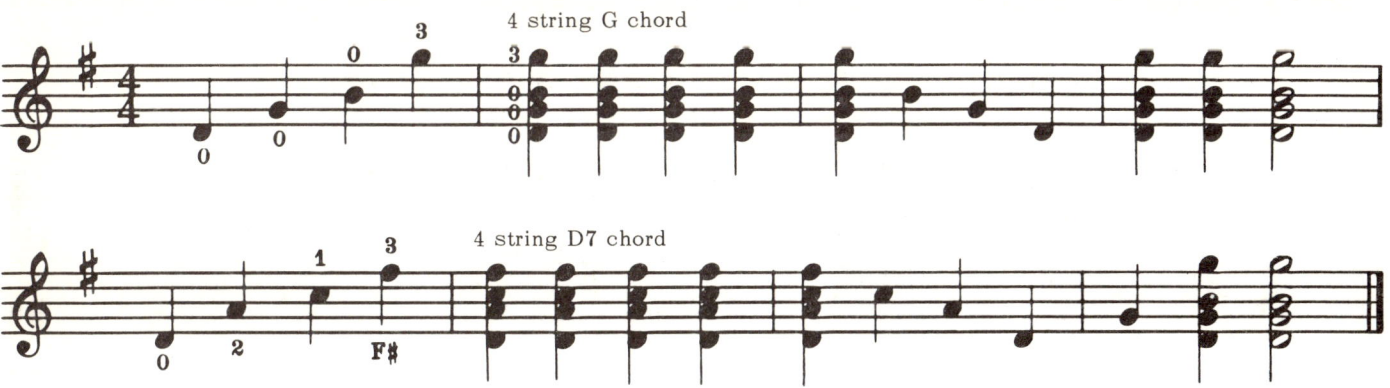

swingin' an' pickin' in the key of g
(using the G and D7 chords)

this old man (PADDY WACK)
(repeat as many times as desired)

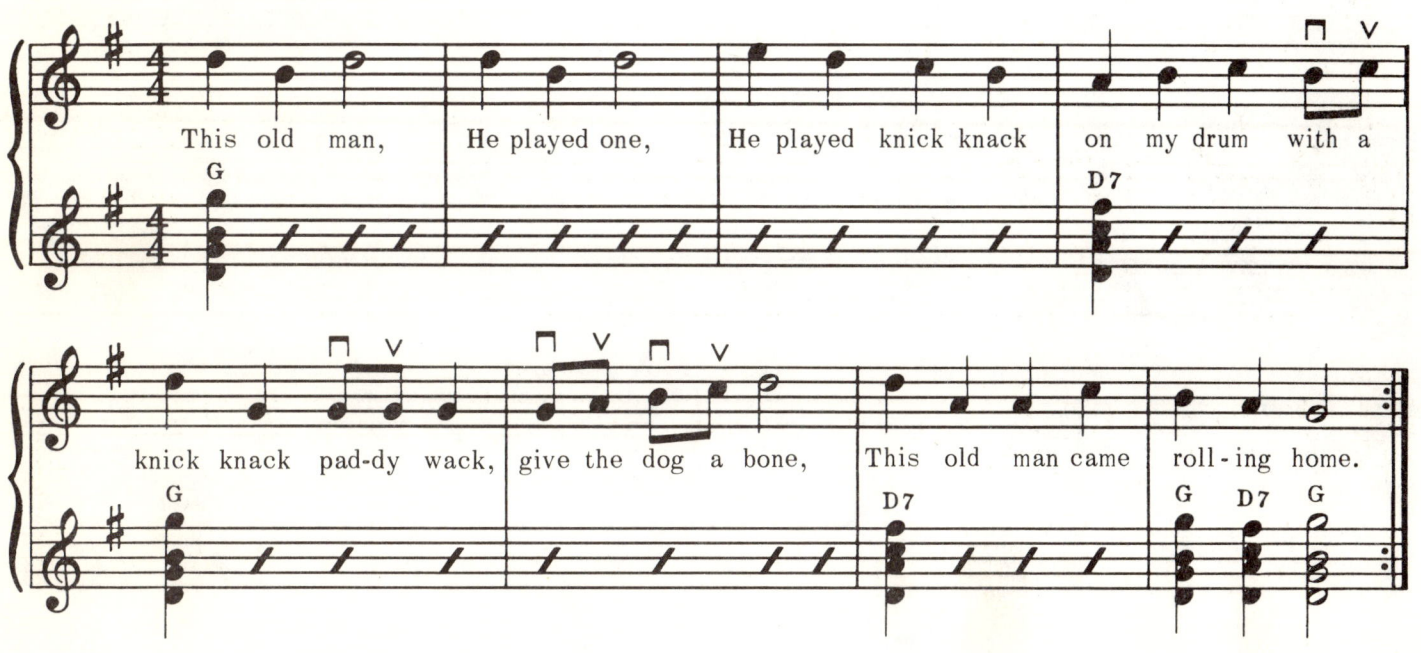

NOTES ON THE D OR 4TH STRING

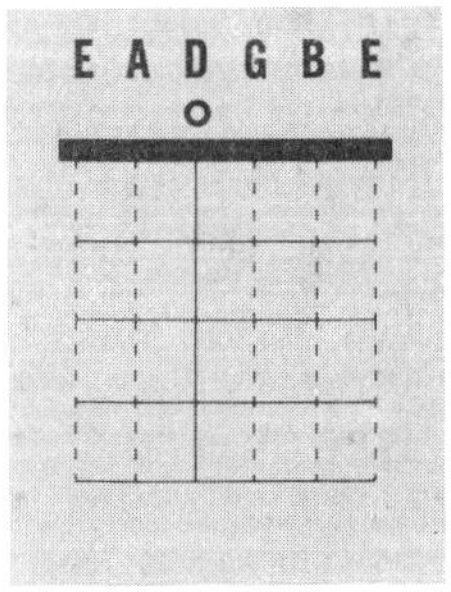

Open **D**

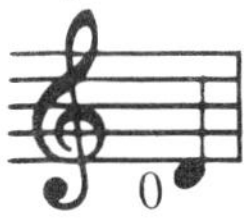

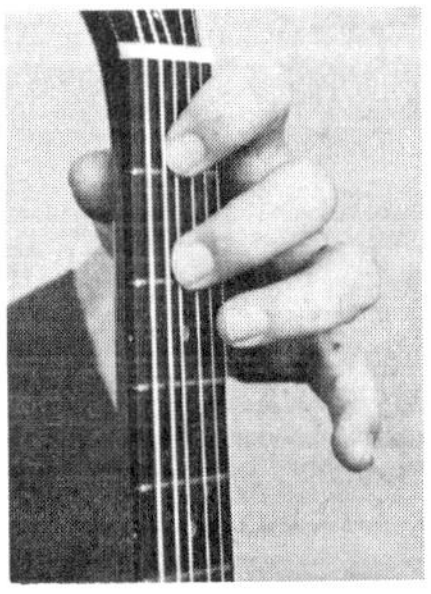

E 2nd Fret

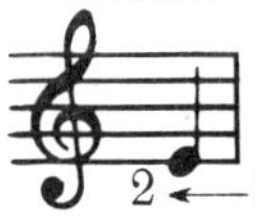

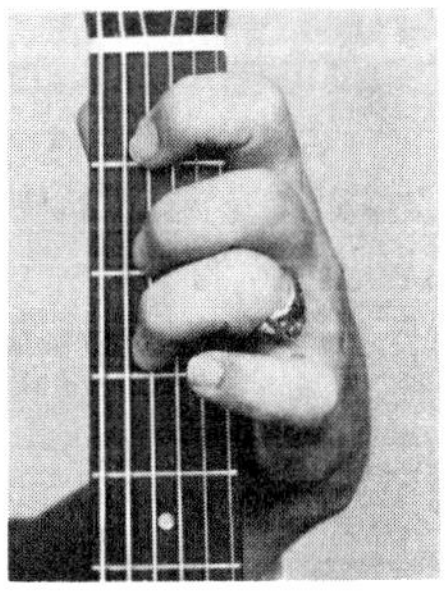

F 3rd Fret

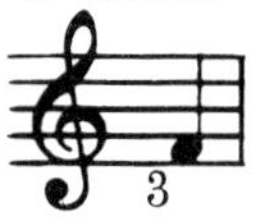

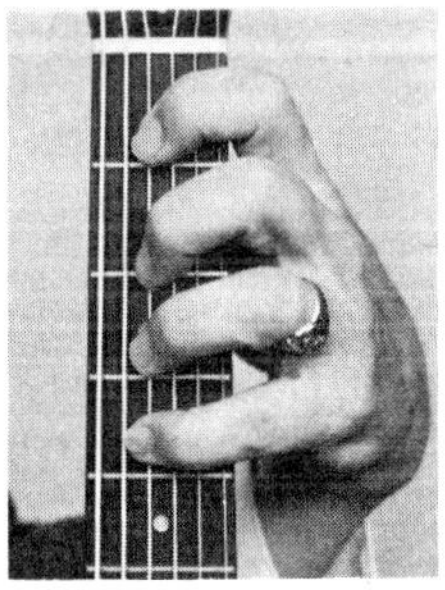

F♯ 4th Fret

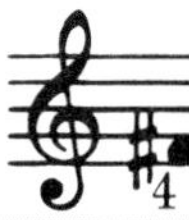

4th STRING EXERCISE (D and E)

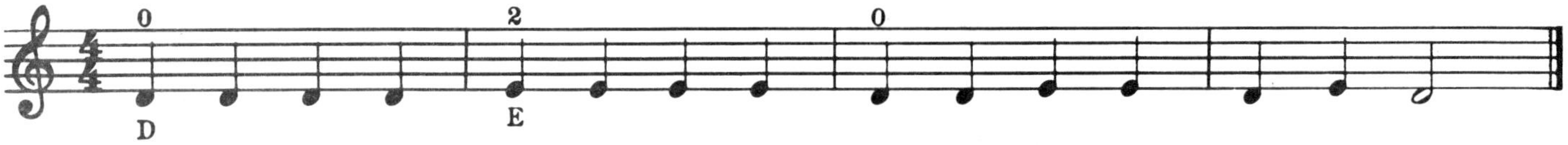

D, E, & F

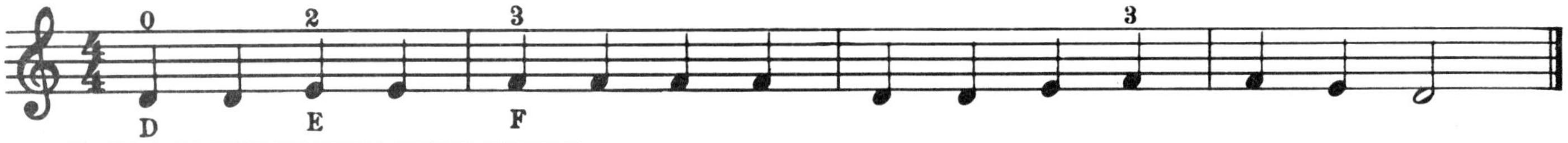

D, E, & F WITH MELODIC SKIPS

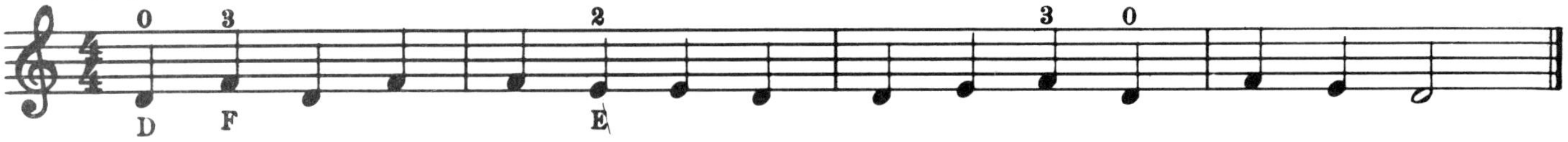

KEY OF G USING A LOWER F♯

long long ago (THIS SONG IS PLAYED ON 4 STRINGS, E, B, G, D)

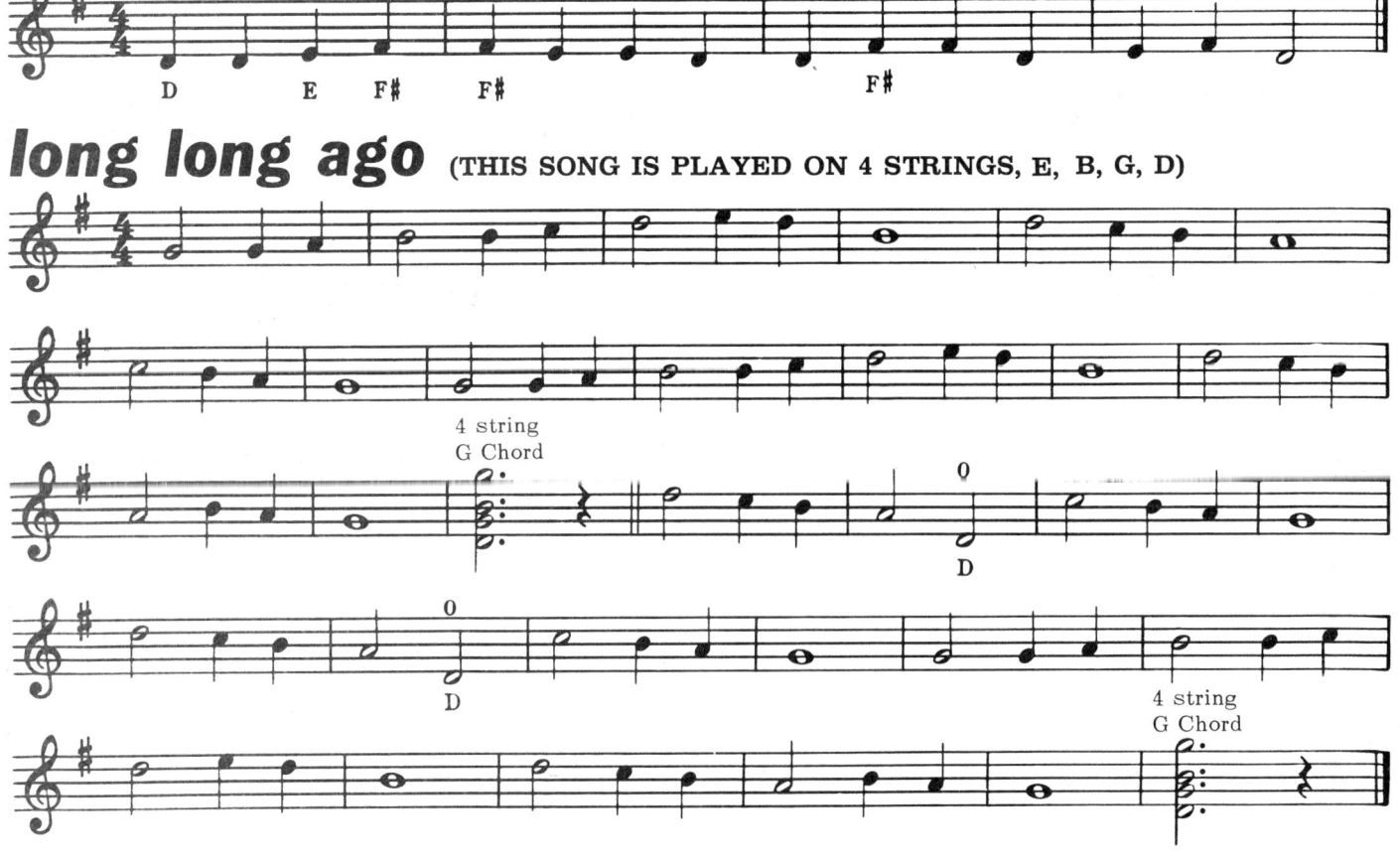

RESTS AND TIED NOTES

Rests

A musical rest is a sign of silence. The length of silence depends on the shape or style of the rest sign.

 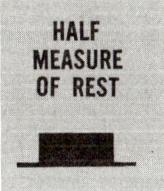 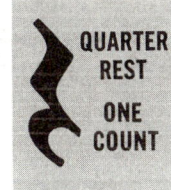 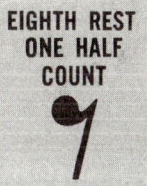

Tied notes

A TIE (⌢) is a curved line uniting two or more notes of the same pitch (same line or space). The tone is sustained (held) for the full value of the tied notes. The second note is not picked . . . . merely sustained.

Note Values and Their Corresponding Rests

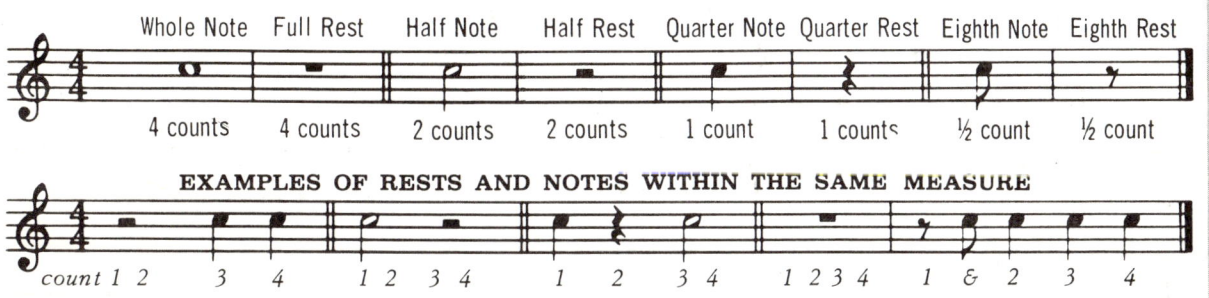

billy boy

2 NEW 4 STRING CHORDS

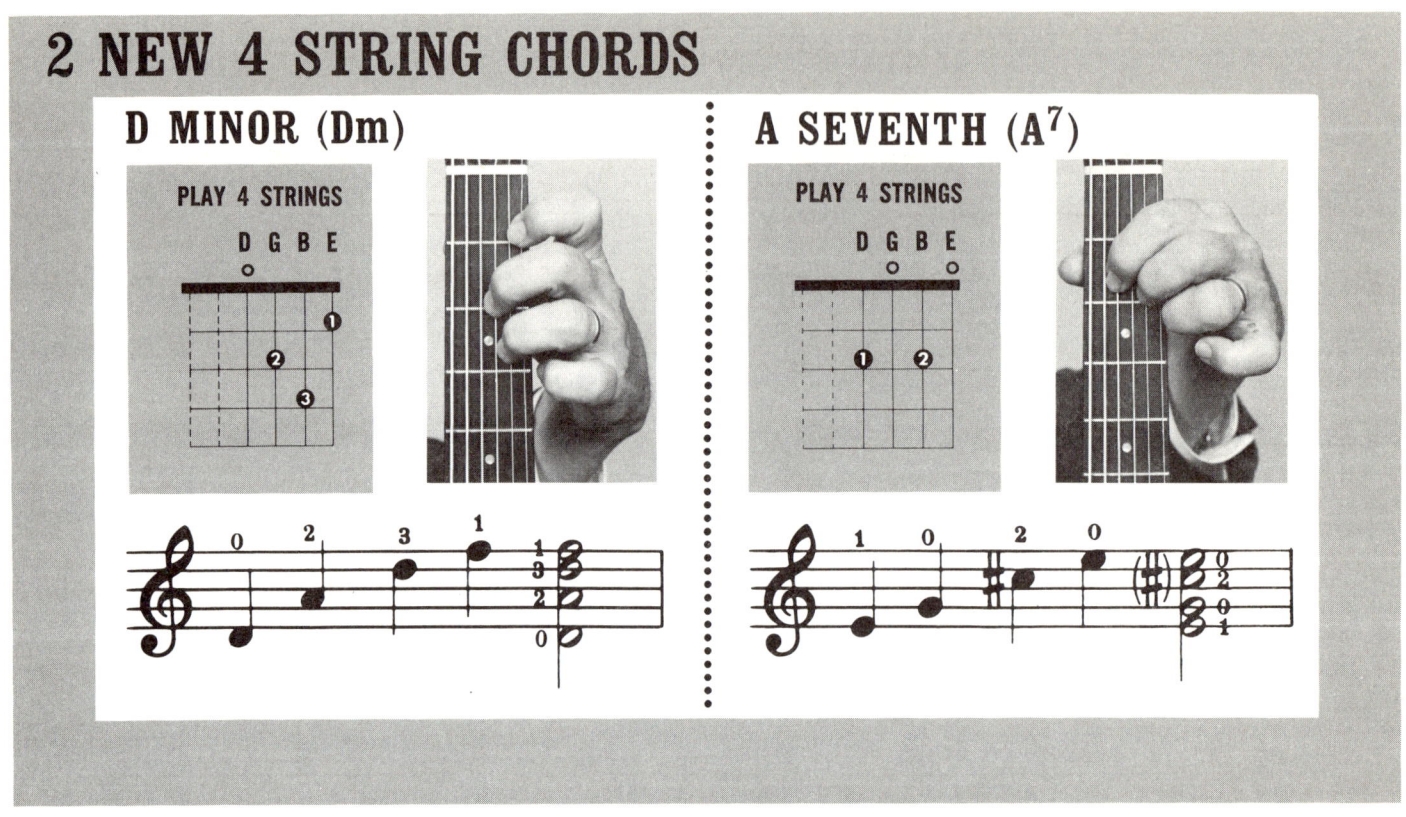

BUILDING THE D MINOR CHORD (composed of 4 notes... D, A, D, F)
Hold each finger in place after playing a note... then play the chord

BUILDING THE A 7th CHORD (composed of 4 notes... E, G, C♯, E)
Hold each finger in place after playing a note... then play the chord

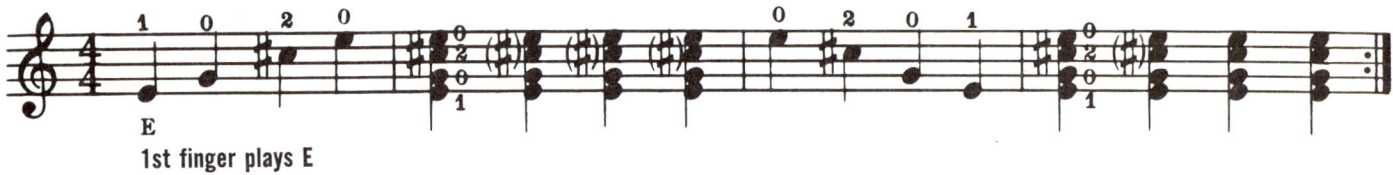

1st finger plays E

a waltz in the minor mood (USING THE D MINOR AND A7th)

WHEN A SHARP IS SHOWN IN PARENTHESIS (♯) IT IS A REMINDER TO USE THE SHARP AGAIN IN THAT MEASURE

This Stephen Foster melody should be counted carefully. Try the practice measures several times (counting aloud) before playing the song.

oh, susanna

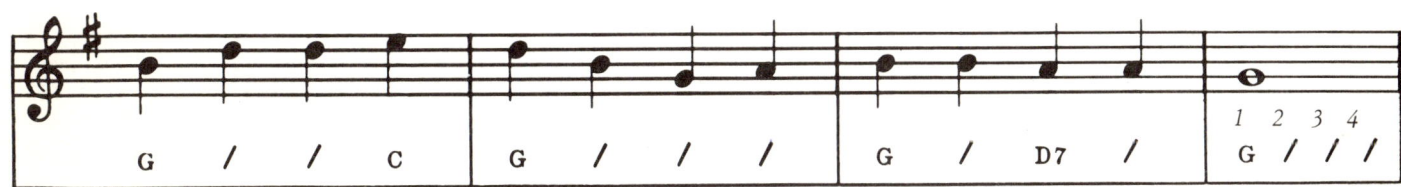

can can

Offenbach

A NEW NOTE - HIGH A

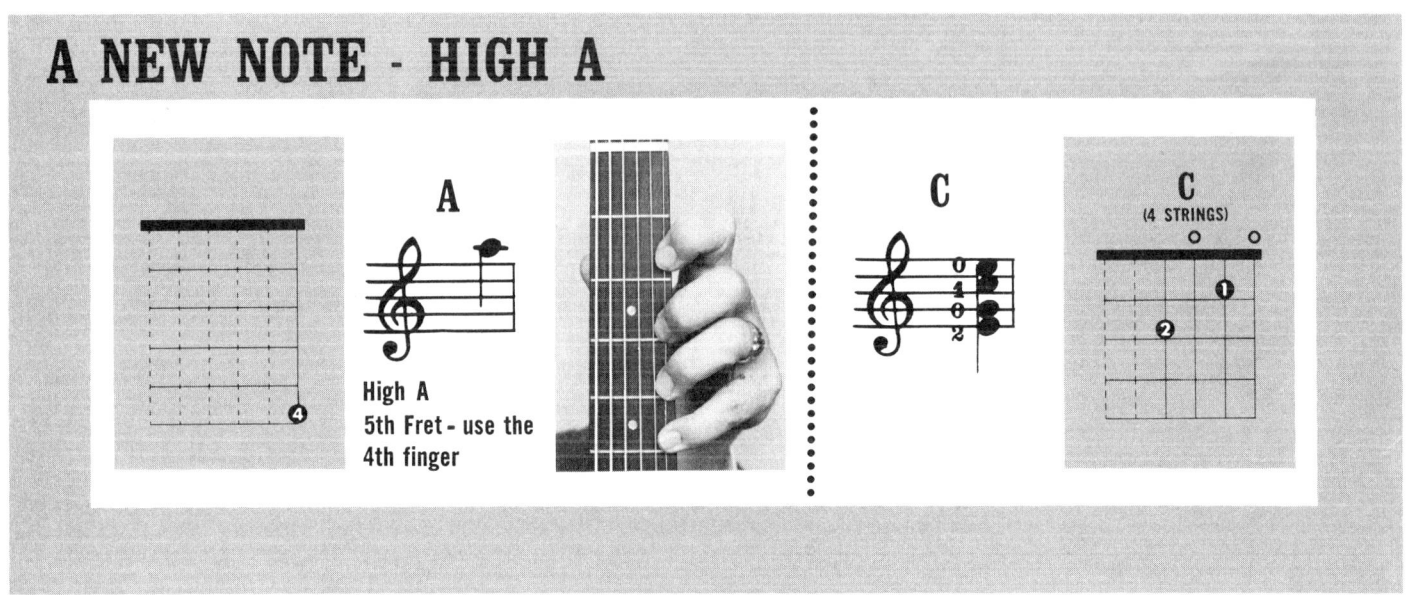

High A
5th Fret - use the 4th finger

C (4 STRINGS)

there is a tavern in the town

This song should be looked over carefully before you start to play. Watch for these features:

1. Key of G ... all F's are sharp.
2. 4/4 time ... only 1 count in 1st measure.
3. There are C♯'s (accidentals).
4. Tied notes.
5. High A is played twice.
6. Dotted quarter notes ... 1½ counts.
7. Eighth notes ... ½ count.
8. 2 chords in one measure.
9. Divided measure ... part of the measure on each page.
10. Two page song.
11. NATURAL F ... (F♯ cancelled for the measure)

28

THREE NEW CHORDS

A minor

Am

E seventh

E7

E

E
or

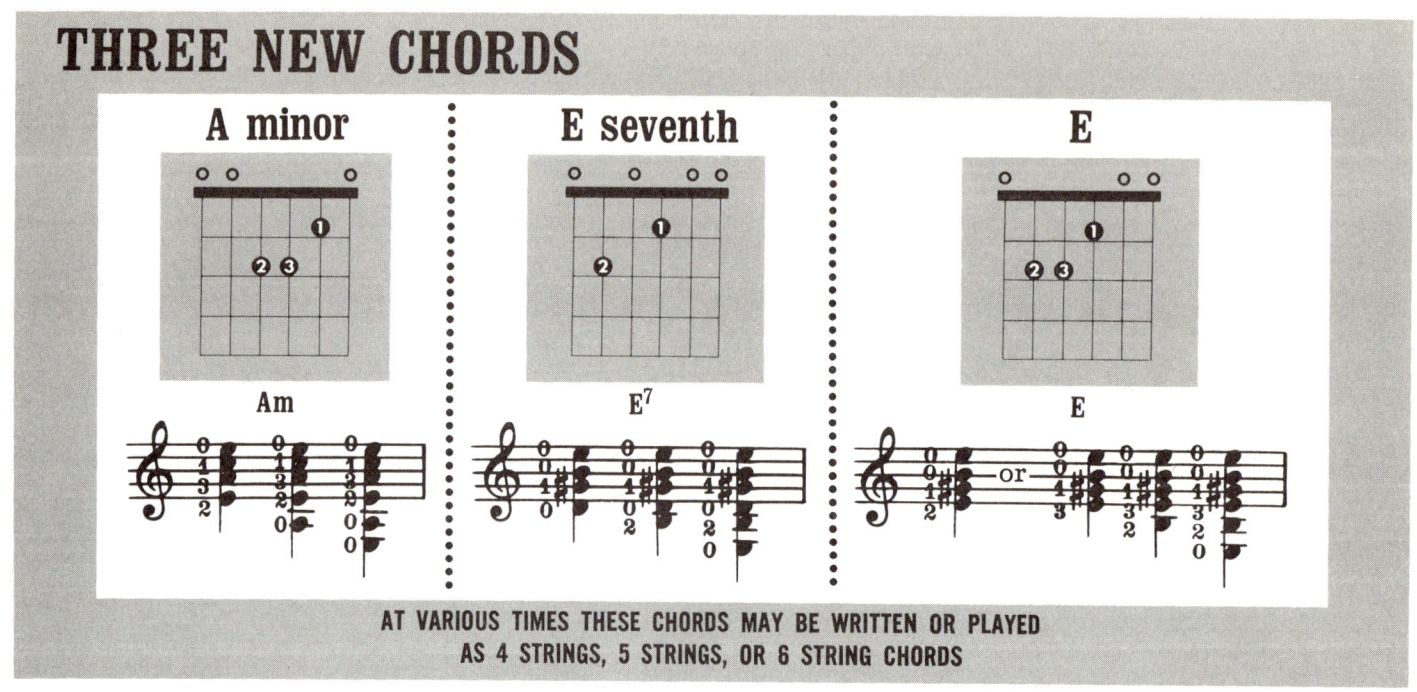

AT VARIOUS TIMES THESE CHORDS MAY BE WRITTEN OR PLAYED
AS 4 STRINGS, 5 STRINGS, OR 6 STRING CHORDS

aura lee

Not fast

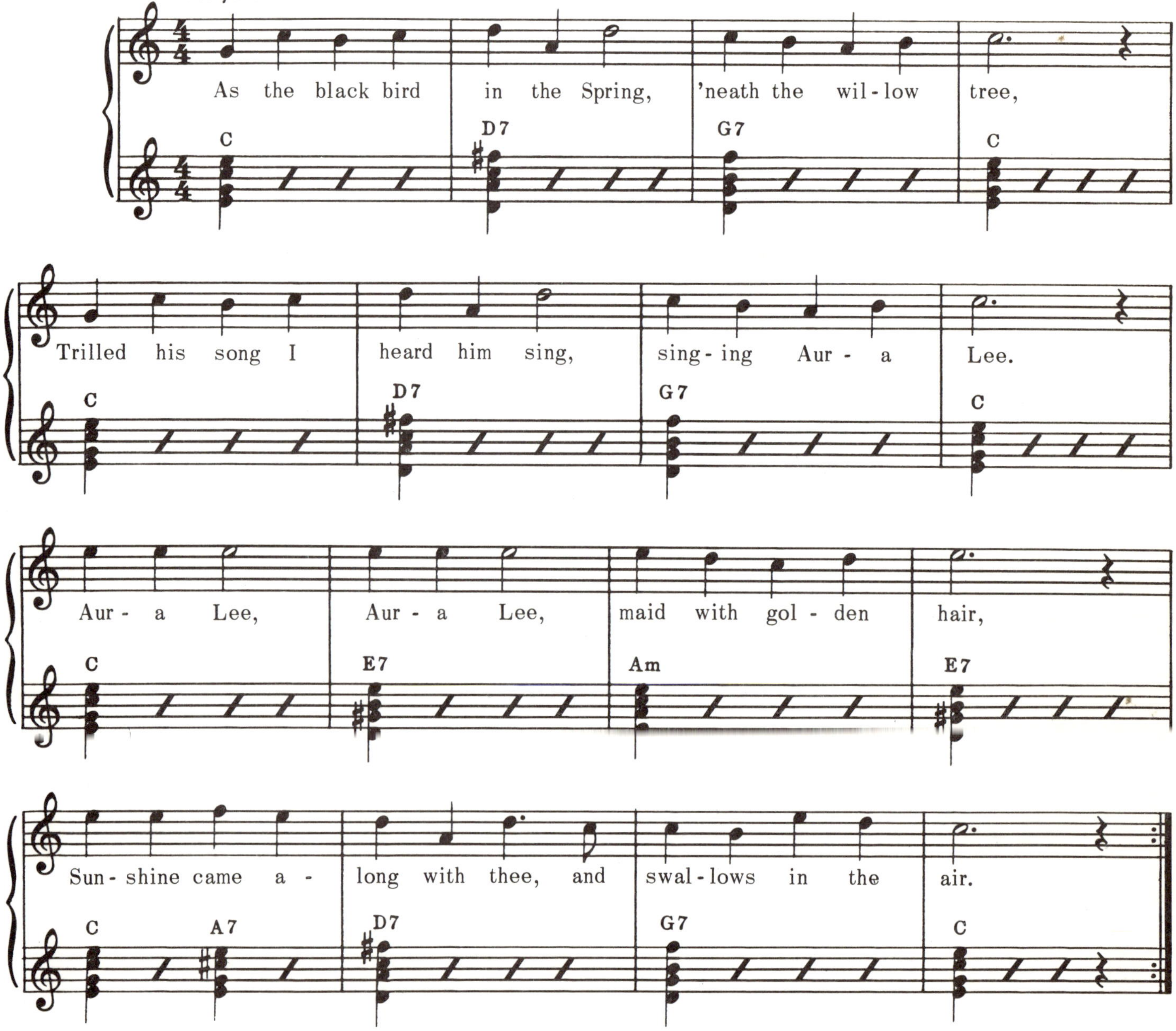

As the black bird in the Spring, 'neath the wil-low tree,
C D7 G7 C
Trilled his song I heard him sing, sing-ing Aur-a Lee.
C D7 G7 C
Aur-a Lee, Aur-a Lee, maid with gol-den hair,
C E7 Am E7
Sun-shine came a-long with thee, and swal-lows in the air.
C A7 D7 G7 C

MID-TERM EXAM

**TRY TO FILL IN AS MANY ANSWERS AS YOU CAN
WITHOUT REFERRING TO THE BOOK....
THEN LOOK FOR ANY ANSWER YOU DO NOT KNOW.**

1. A music staff is composed of _____ lines and _____ spaces.
2. Name the lines. _____
3. Name the spaces. _____
4. This (𝄞) is called a _____
5. An added line above or below the staff is called a _____ line.
6. This (♯) is called a _____. It _____ a note by _____.
7. This (♭) is called a _____. It _____ a note by _____.
8. This (♮) is called a _____. It _____ a sharp or flat.
9. The top number in a time signature tells the _____ of counts in a _____.
10. The lower number in a time signature tells the kind of a note that gets _____ count.
11. In 4/4 time a whole note (o) should be held for _____ counts.
12. In 4/4 time a half note (♩) should be held for _____ counts.
13. The musical alphabet is composed of _____ letters. They are _____.
14. The final double bar in a song is always (light . . . dark). Underline one answer.
15. When a piece begins with an incomplete measure, we find the rest of the counts in the _____ measure.
16. D. C. is the abbreviation for _____. It means _____
17. Fine means _____.
18. This mark (⊓) means _____.
19. Rests are signs of _____.
20. When two notes are tied (♩‿♩) should the second note be picked? _____

FOR TEACHER'S USE

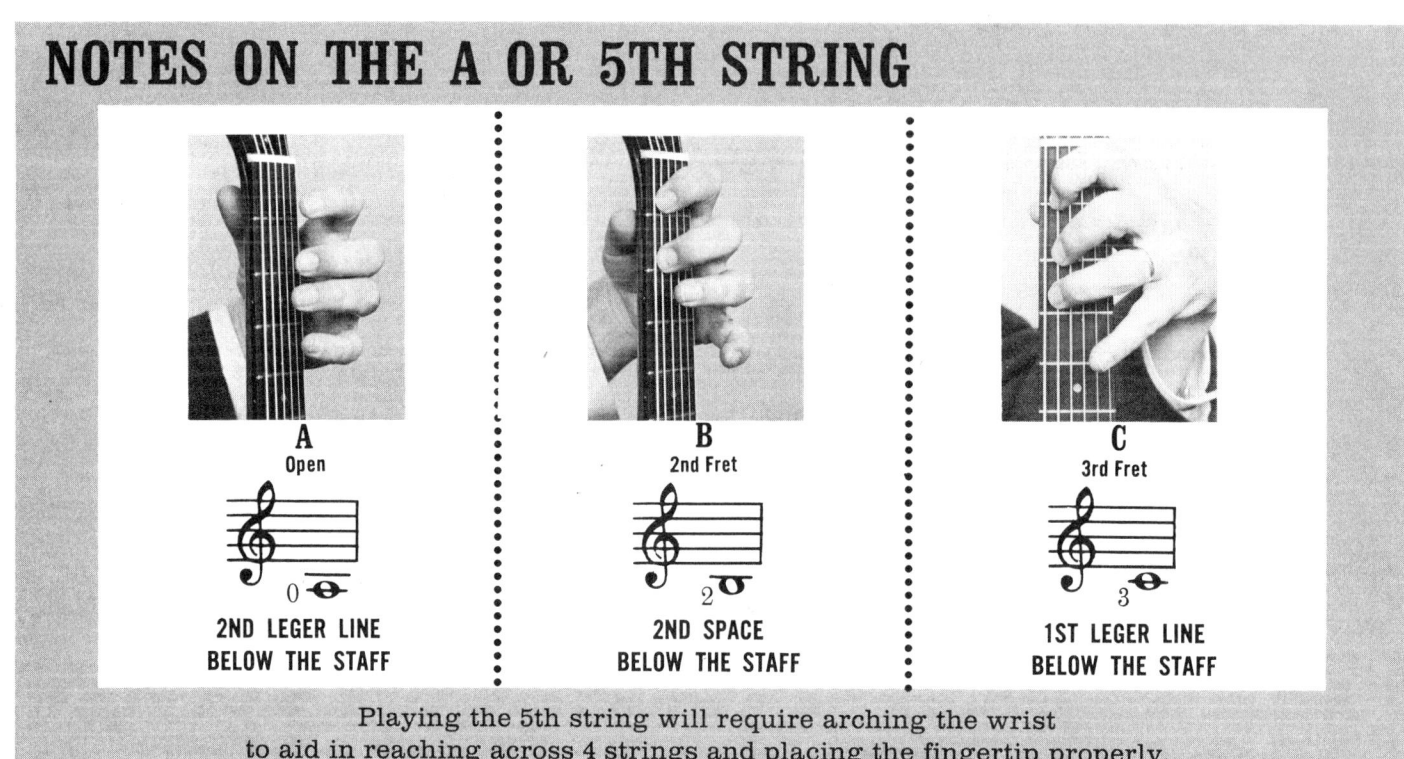
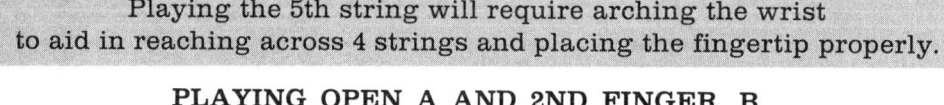

coming 'round the mountain

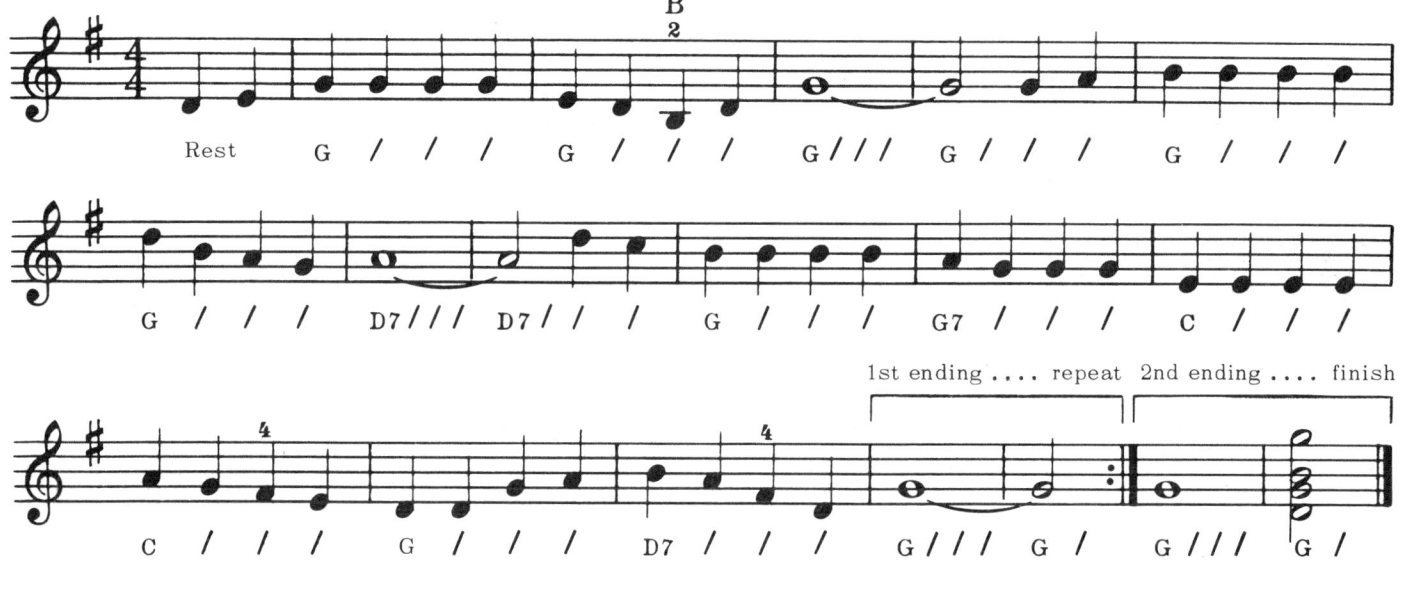

patriotic song

RHYTHM AND PICKING EXERCISE FOR CAMPTOWN RACES

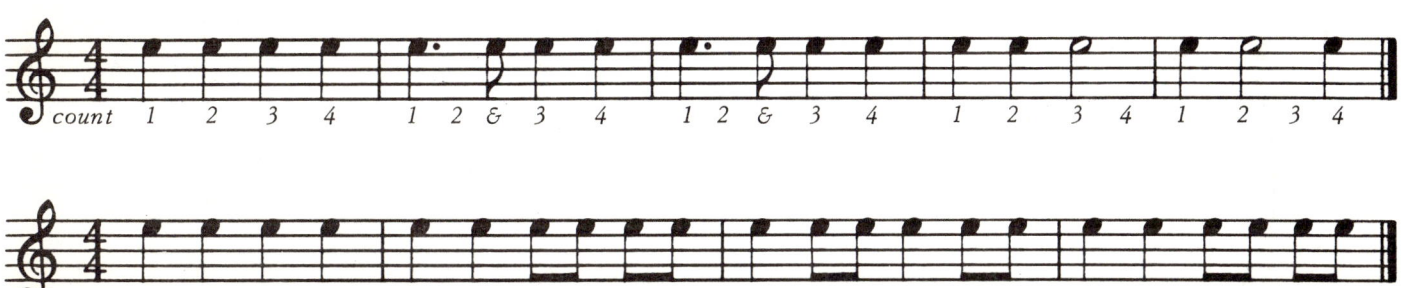

camptown races

Stephen Foster

2 CHORDS

G
(6 STRINGS)

Em
(6 STRINGS)

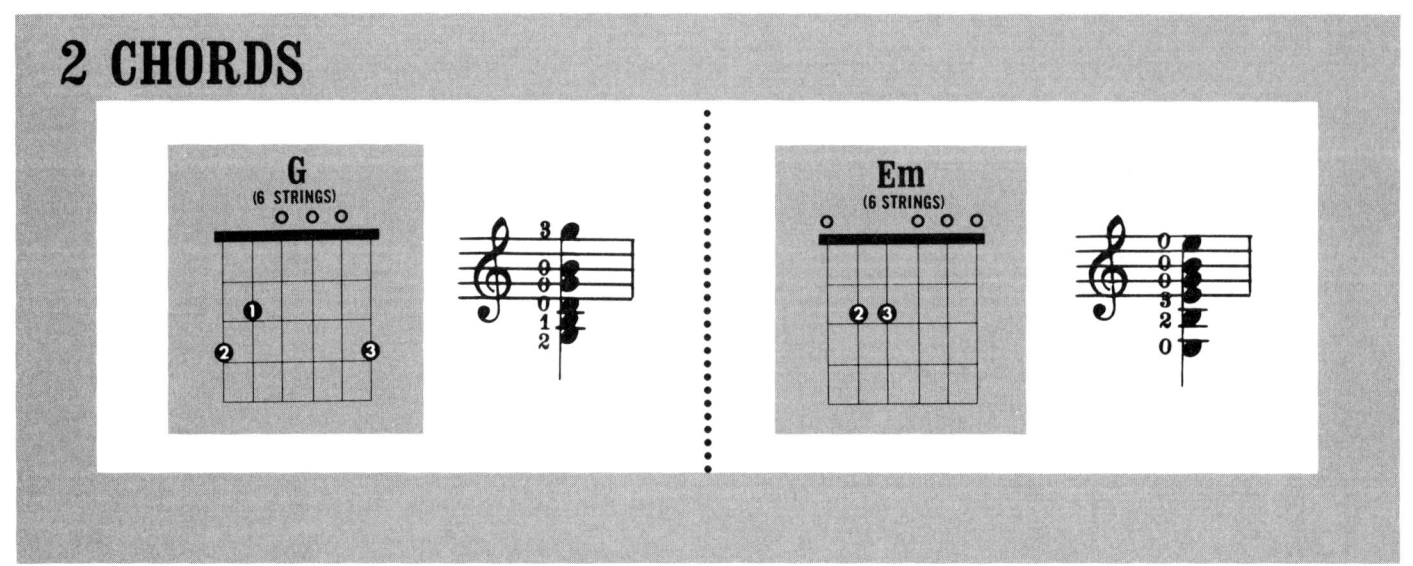

sweet betsy from pike

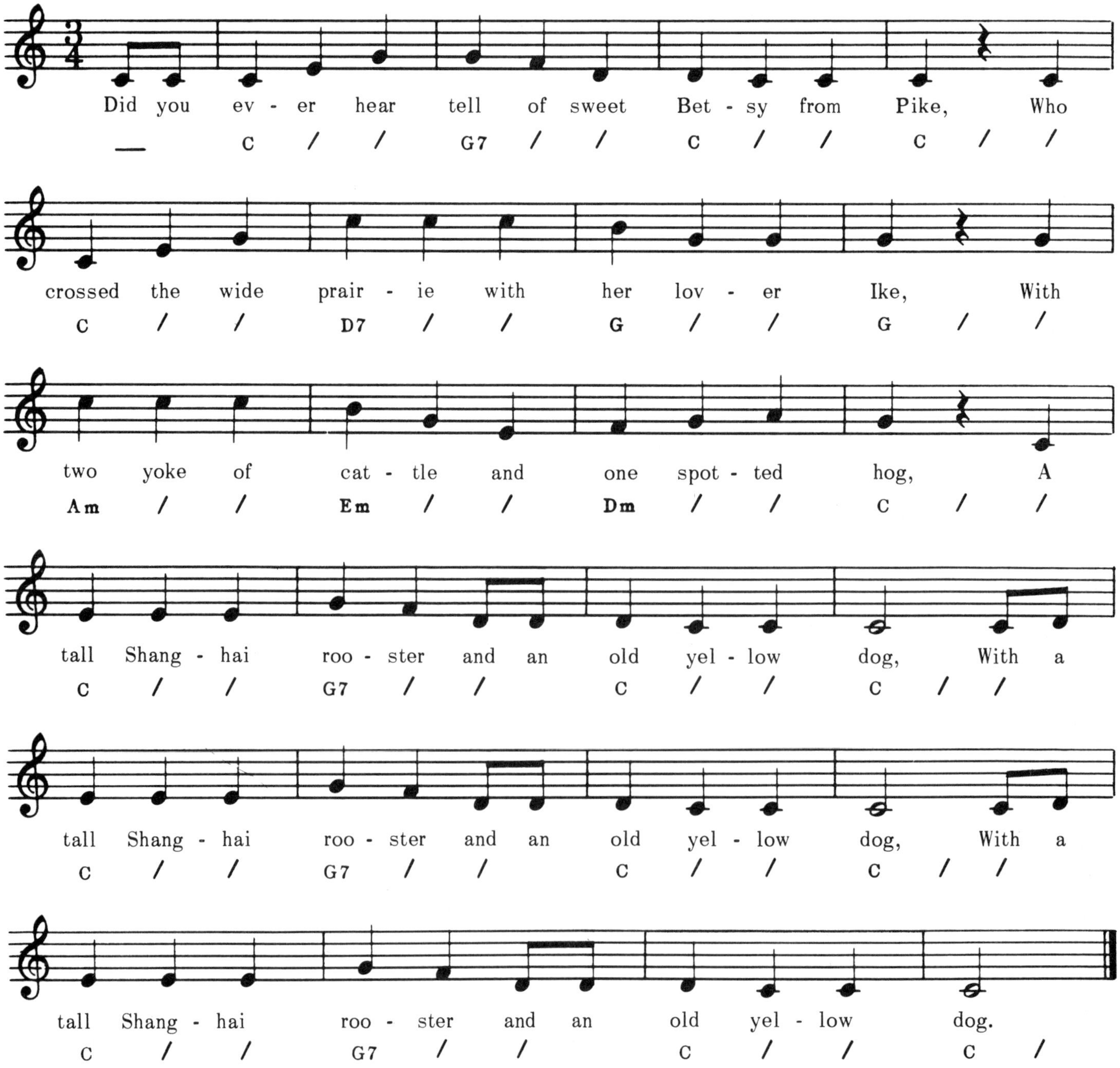

Did you ev - er hear tell of sweet Bet - sy from Pike, Who
— C / / G7 / / C / / C / /
crossed the wide prair - ie with her lov - er Ike, With
C / / D7 / / G / / G / /
two yoke of cat - tle and one spot - ted hog, A
Am / / Em / / Dm / / C / /
tall Shang - hai roo - ster and an old yel - low dog, With a
C / / G7 / / C / / C / /
tall Shang - hai roo - ster and an old yel - low dog, With a
C / / G7 / / C / / C / /
tall Shang - hai roo - ster and an old yel - low dog.
C / / G7 / / C / / C /

ACCENT MARK >

 This mark (>) above or below a note means the note should be emphasized ... (played louder). Melody notes should always be well accented. Chords that are used as fill-ins should always be played softly.

By combining the melody and chords the student can create the effect of two guitars.

Watch for: 1. Incomplete measures. 2. Accidentals (A♯). 3. Eighth notes. 4. Accents.

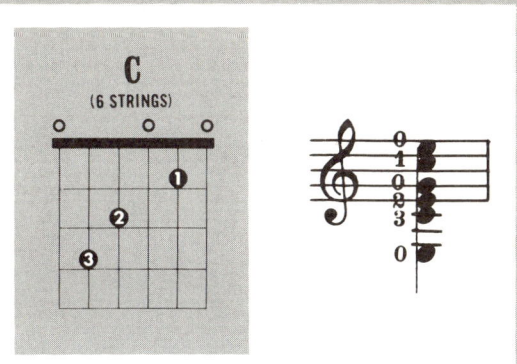

The eighth note chords may be played **down and up** or **all down** strokes.

the one man band

little brown jug

i'm a yankee doodle dandy

George M. Cohan

RHYTHM AND PICKING EXERCISE

| PAUSE OR HOLD | 𝄐 | This sign (𝄐) placed above or below a note indicates that the performer may hold the note as long as desired. |

jimmy crack corn

when the saints go marching in

38

the jolly farmer

Schumann

SCALE OF C

The scale of C begins on C and ends on C. (C, D, E, F, G, A, B, C)

The key signature for the key of C is shown by the absence of sharps or flats.

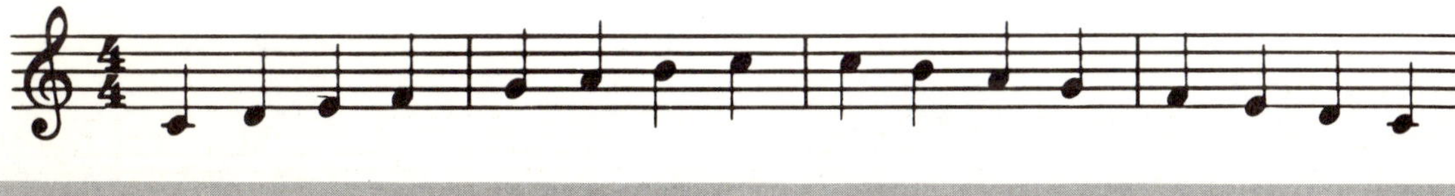

julida polka

Not slow

REMINDER

C

E7

Am

chiapanecas (GAILY, NOW GAILY, WE ALL CLAP HANDS)

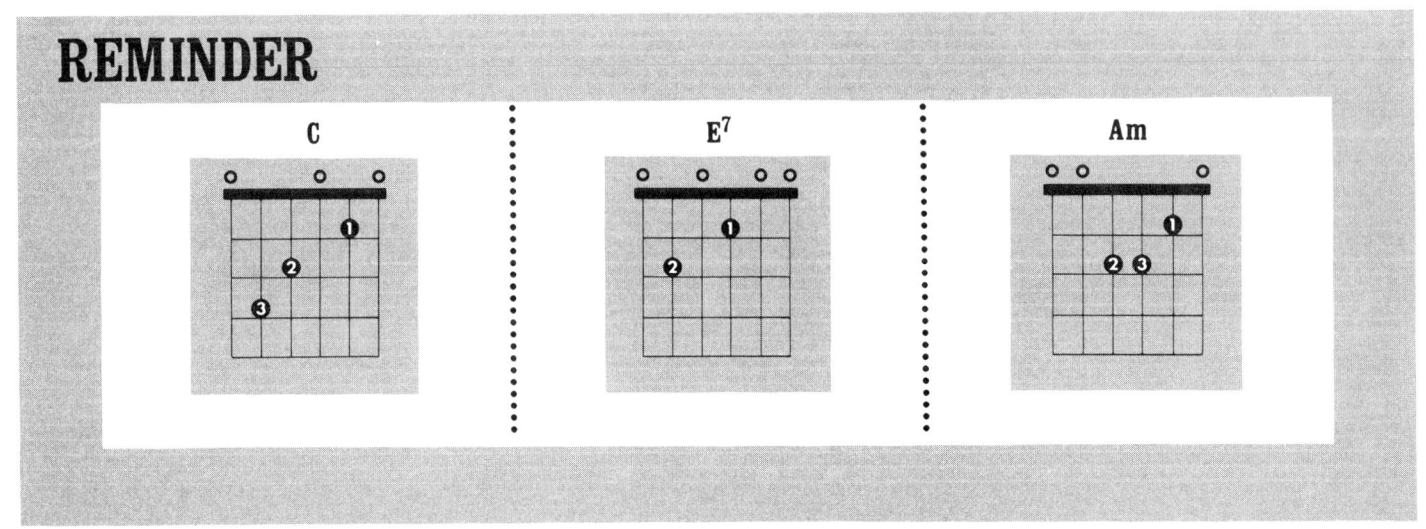

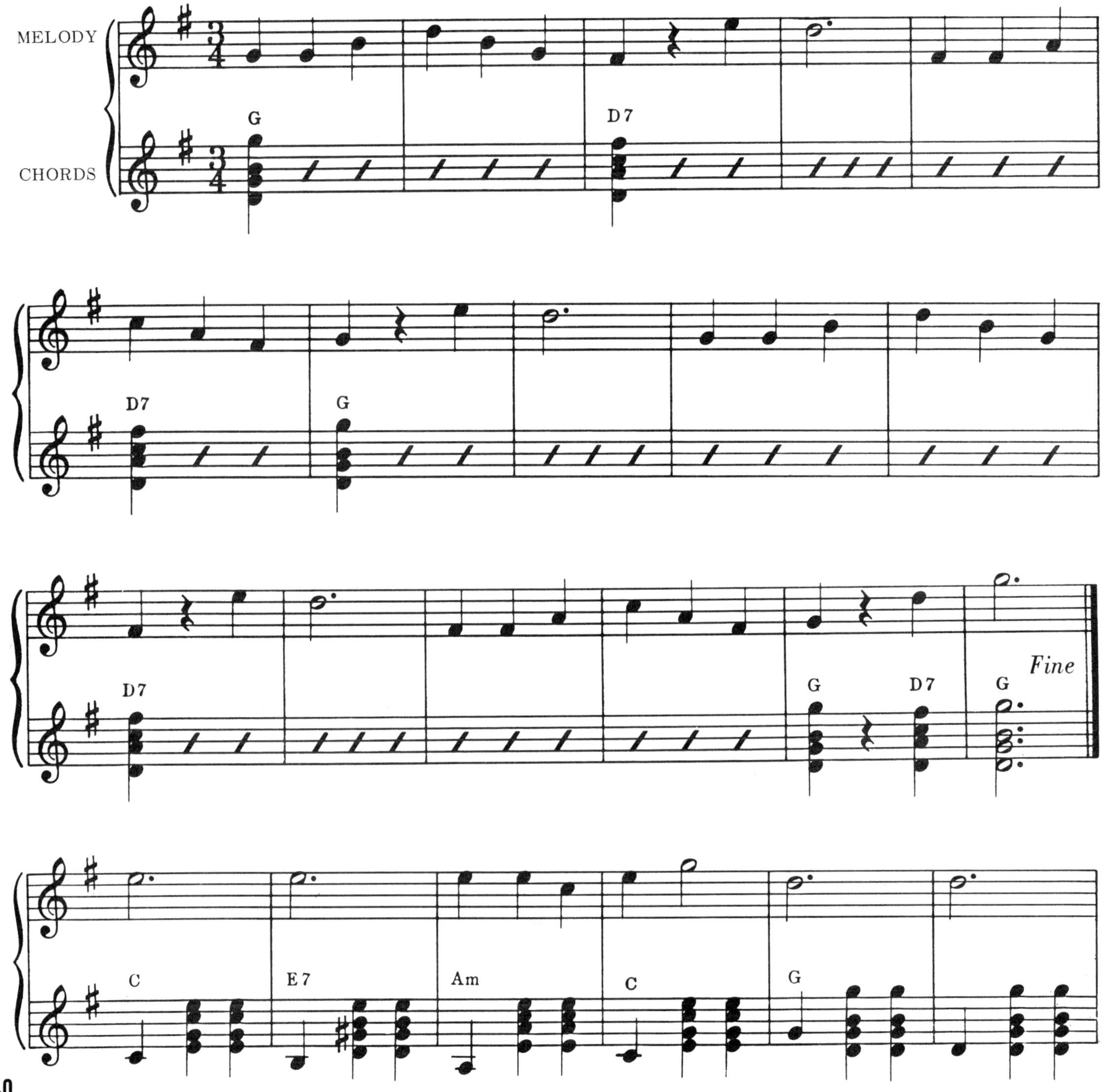

NOTES ON THE E OR 6TH STRING

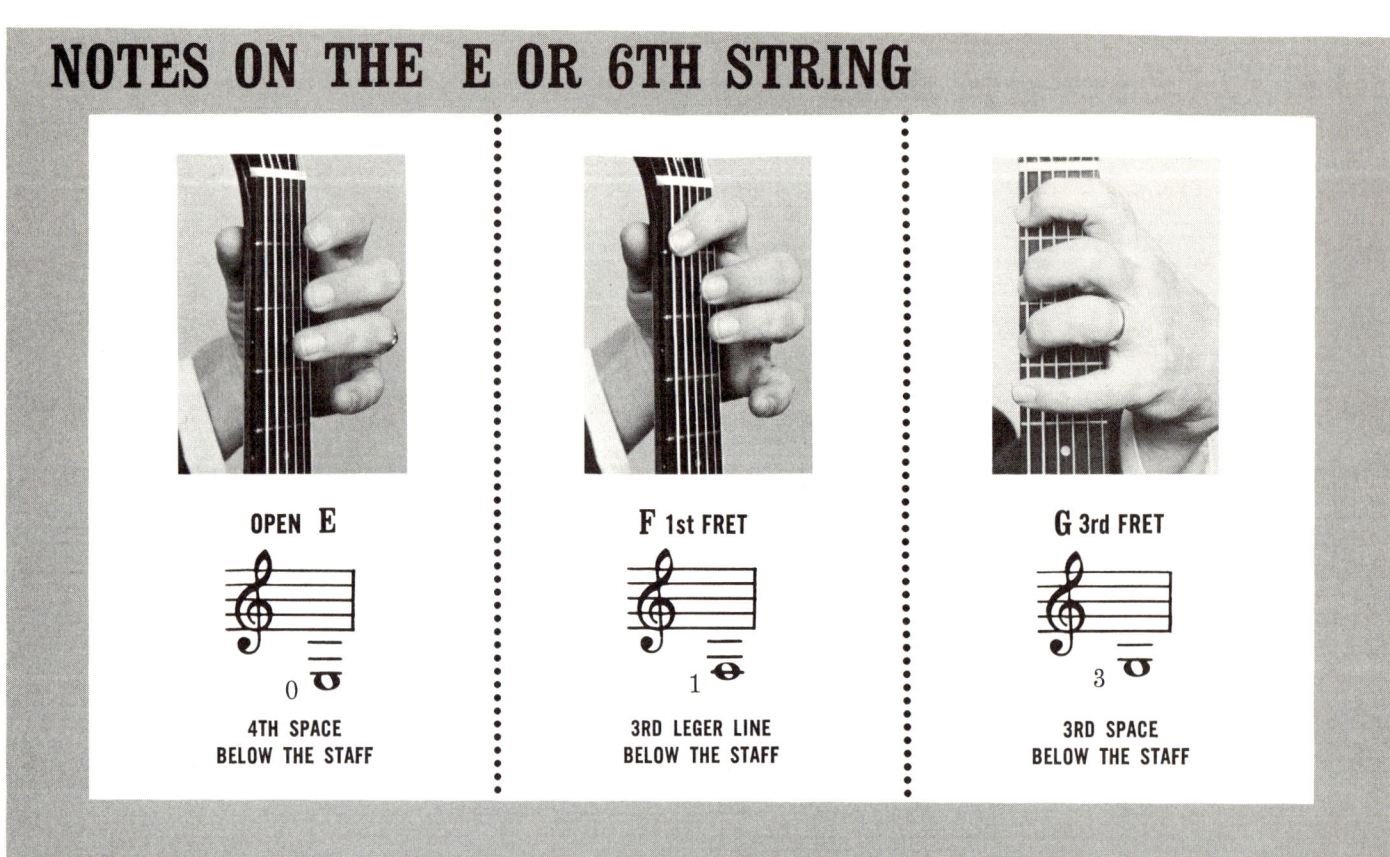

(OPEN E AND FIRST FINGER F)

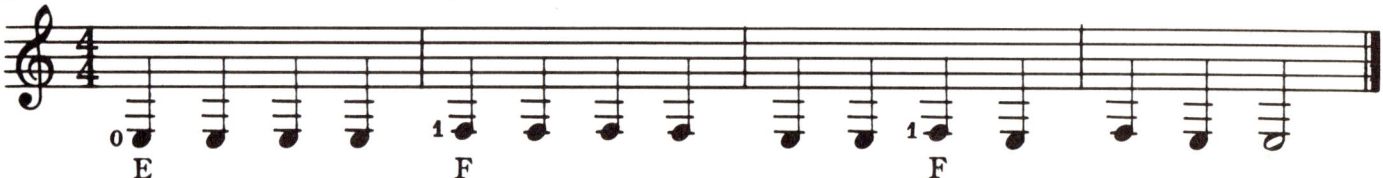

(OPEN E – FIRST FINGER F – THIRD FINGER G)

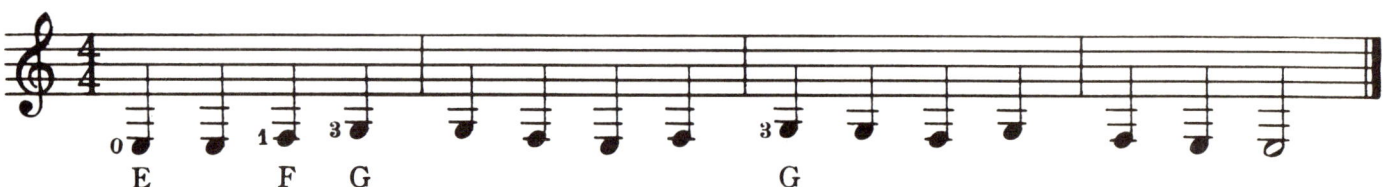

PLAYING E, F, G, WITH MELODIC SKIPS

looby lou

the volga boatman (NOTES ON THE 4th, 5th AND 6th STRINGS)

THE ALTERNATE BASS

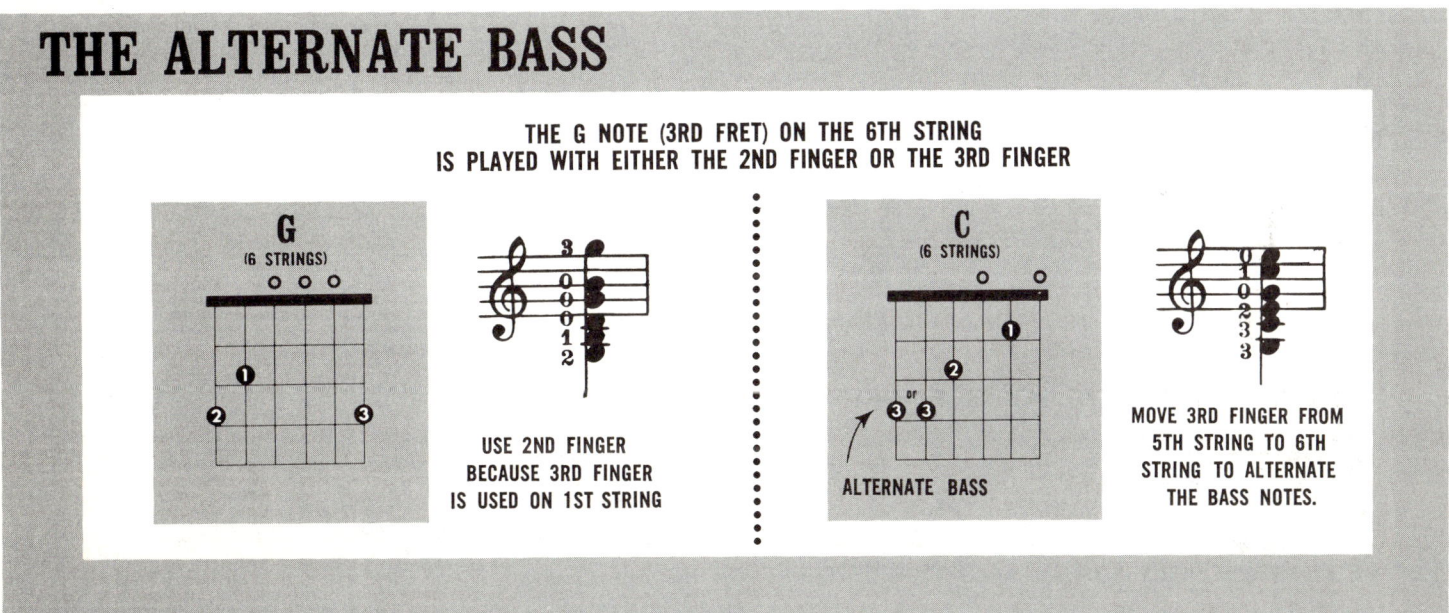

BASS RUNS COMBINED WITH BASS NOTES AND CHORDS

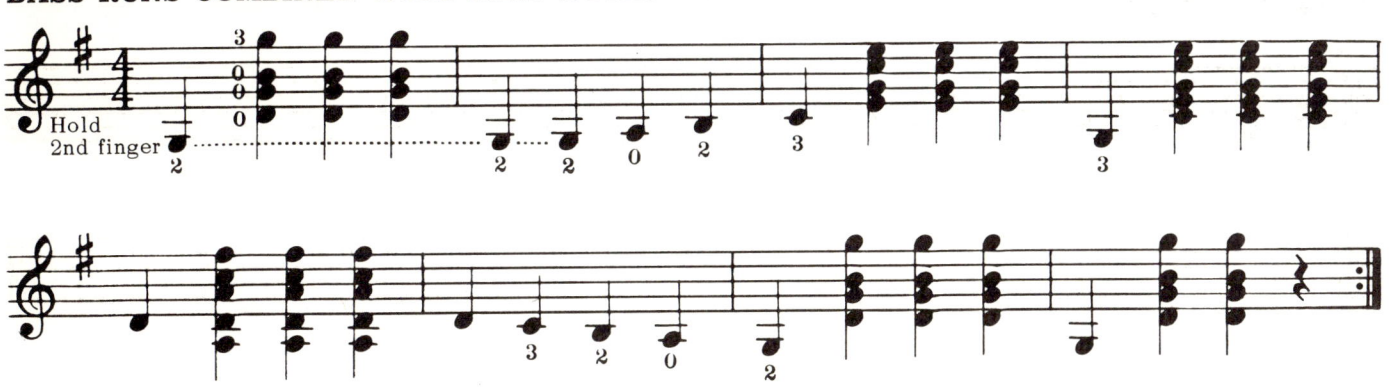

43

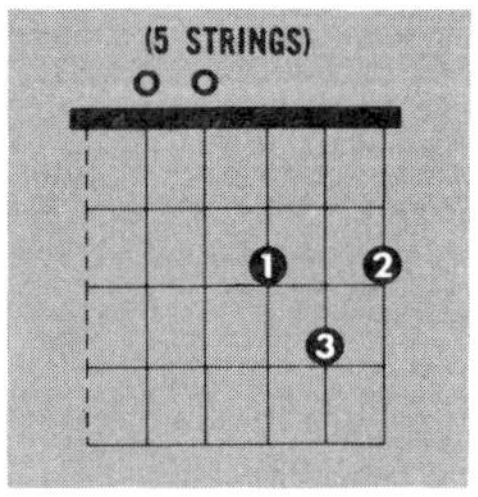

D CHORD

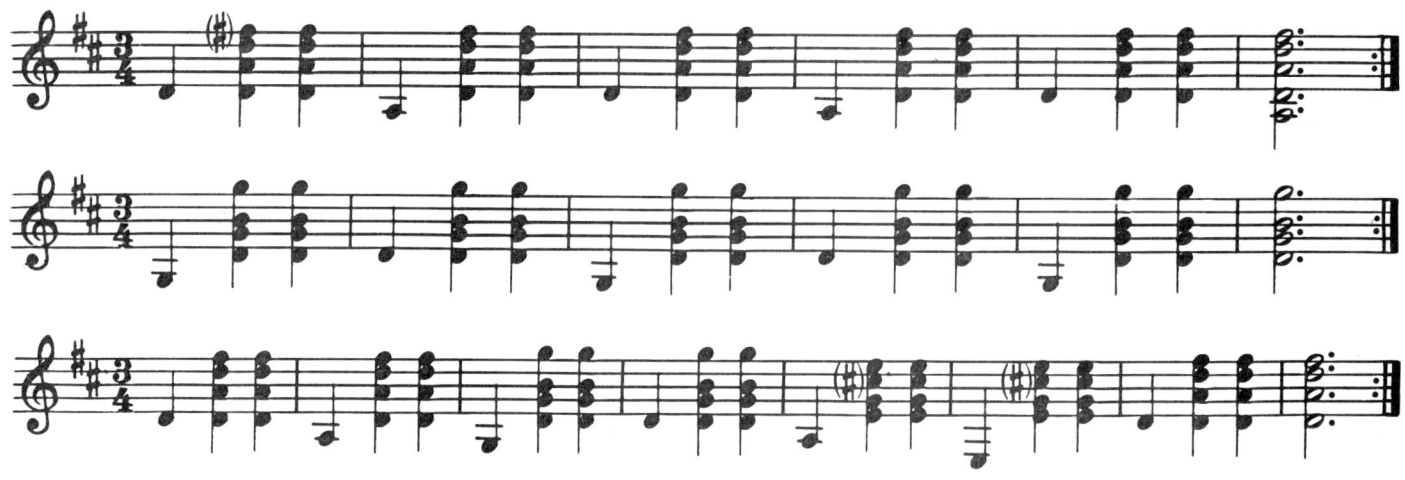

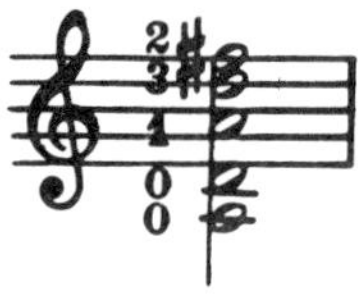

USE 4TH OR 5TH STRING FOR BASS NOTE.

WITH ALTERNATE BASS

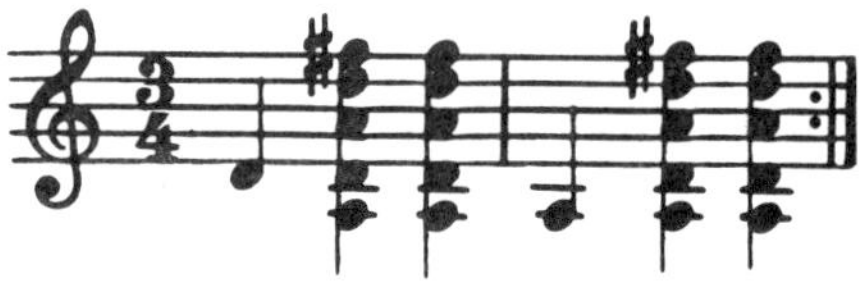

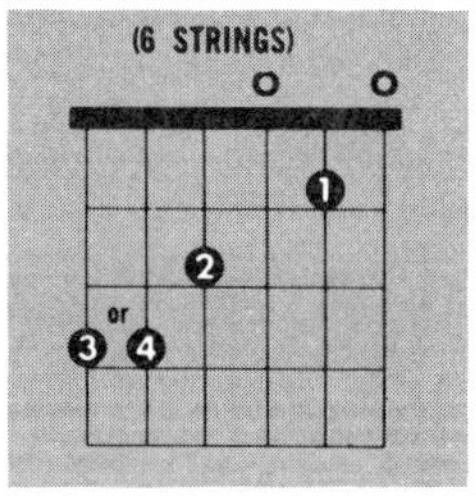

C CHORD

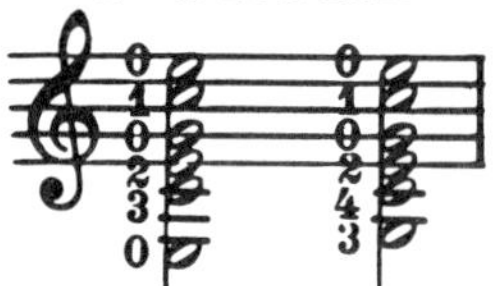

USE 5TH OR 6TH STRING FOR BASS NOTE.

WITH ALTERNATE BASS

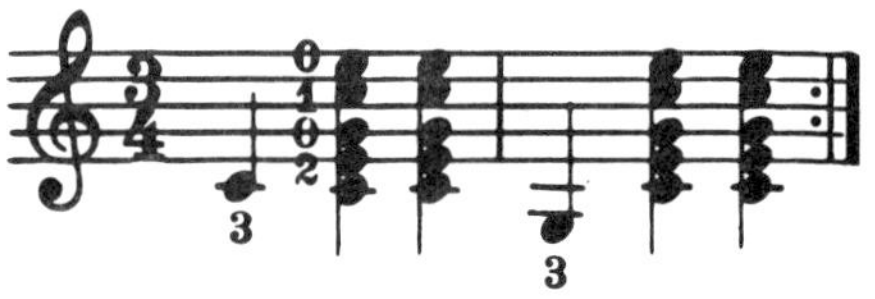

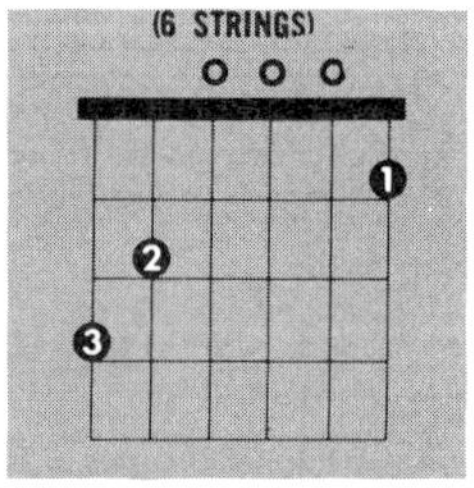

G^7 CHORD

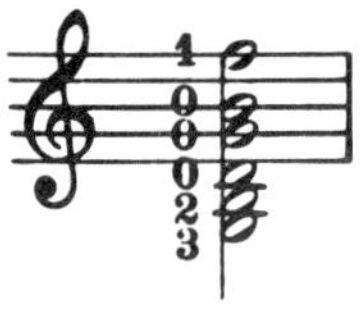

USE 6TH OR 4TH STRING FOR BASS NOTE.

WITH ALTERNATE BASS

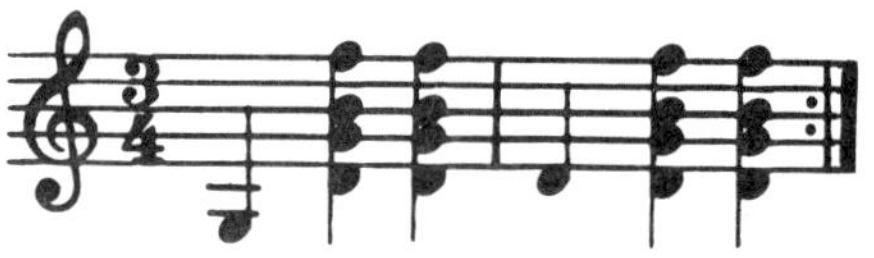

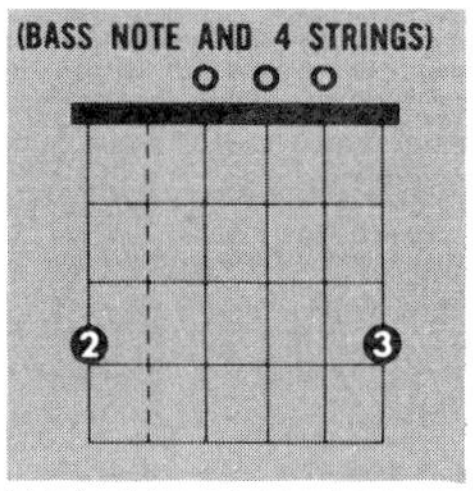

G CHORD

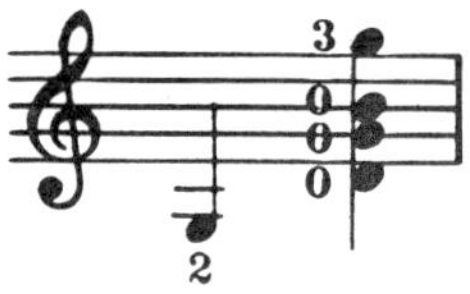

USE 6TH OR 4TH STRING FOR BASS NOTE.

WITH ALTERNATE BASS

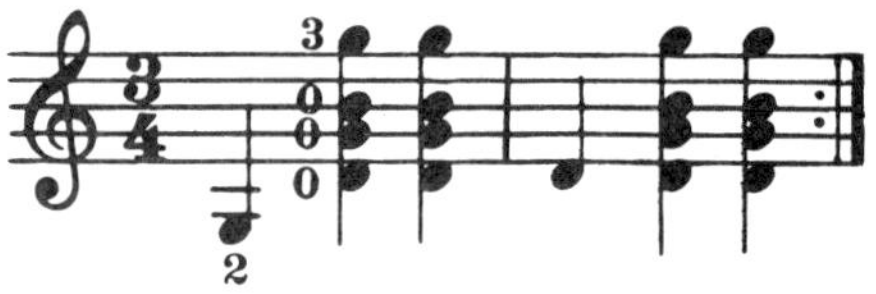

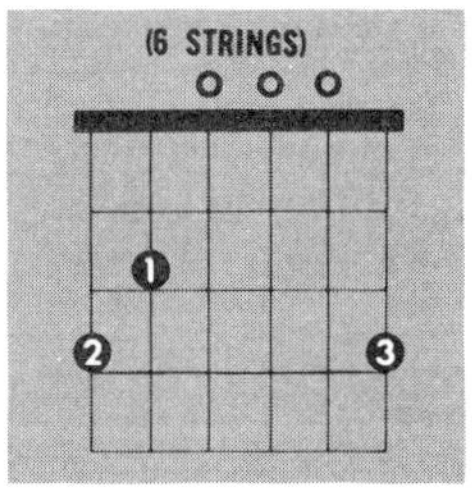

G CHORD

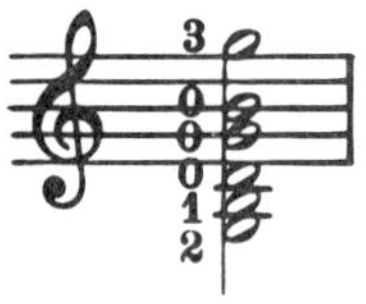

USE 6TH OR 4TH STRING FOR BASS NOTE.

A^7 WITH ALTERNATE BASS

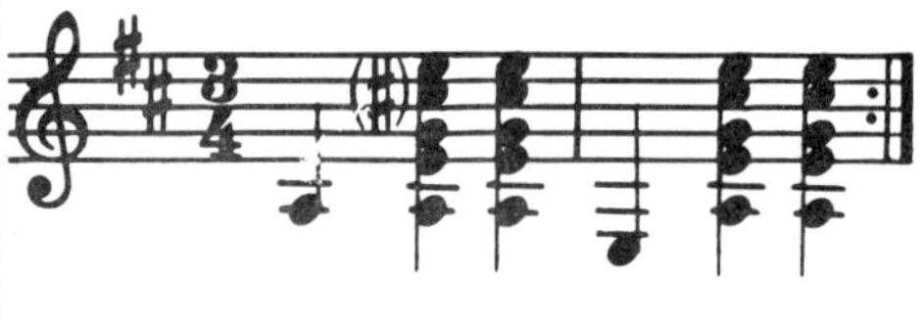

ALTERNATING BASSES AND CHORDS (D) (G) (A7)

KEY OF D

THE KEY SIGNATURE FOR THE KEY OF D IS TWO SHARPS. F♯ and C♯

The scale of D begins on D and ends on D (D, E, F♯, G, A, B, C♯, D)

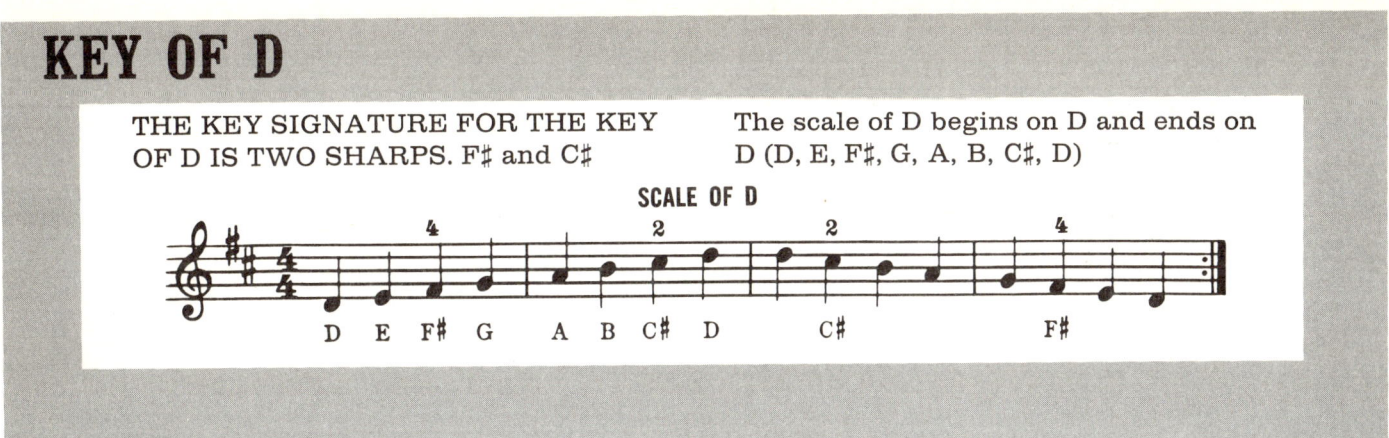

SCALE OF D

4 2 2 4
D E F♯ G A B C♯ D C♯ F♯

cowboy jack

Key of D
MELODY
CHORDS
Out on the lone - ly prai - rie, your true love waits for you, Your true love waits for you Jack, your true love waits for you.
D D G G A7 A7 D D D D G G A7 A7 D D

cuckoo waltz

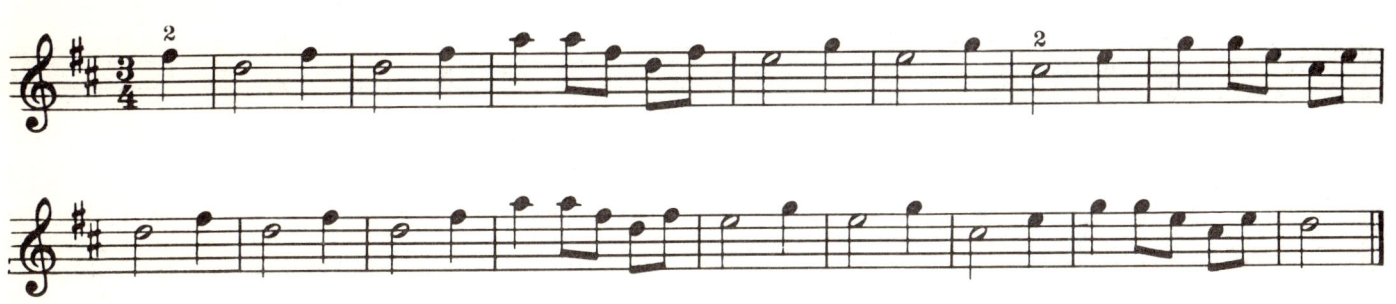

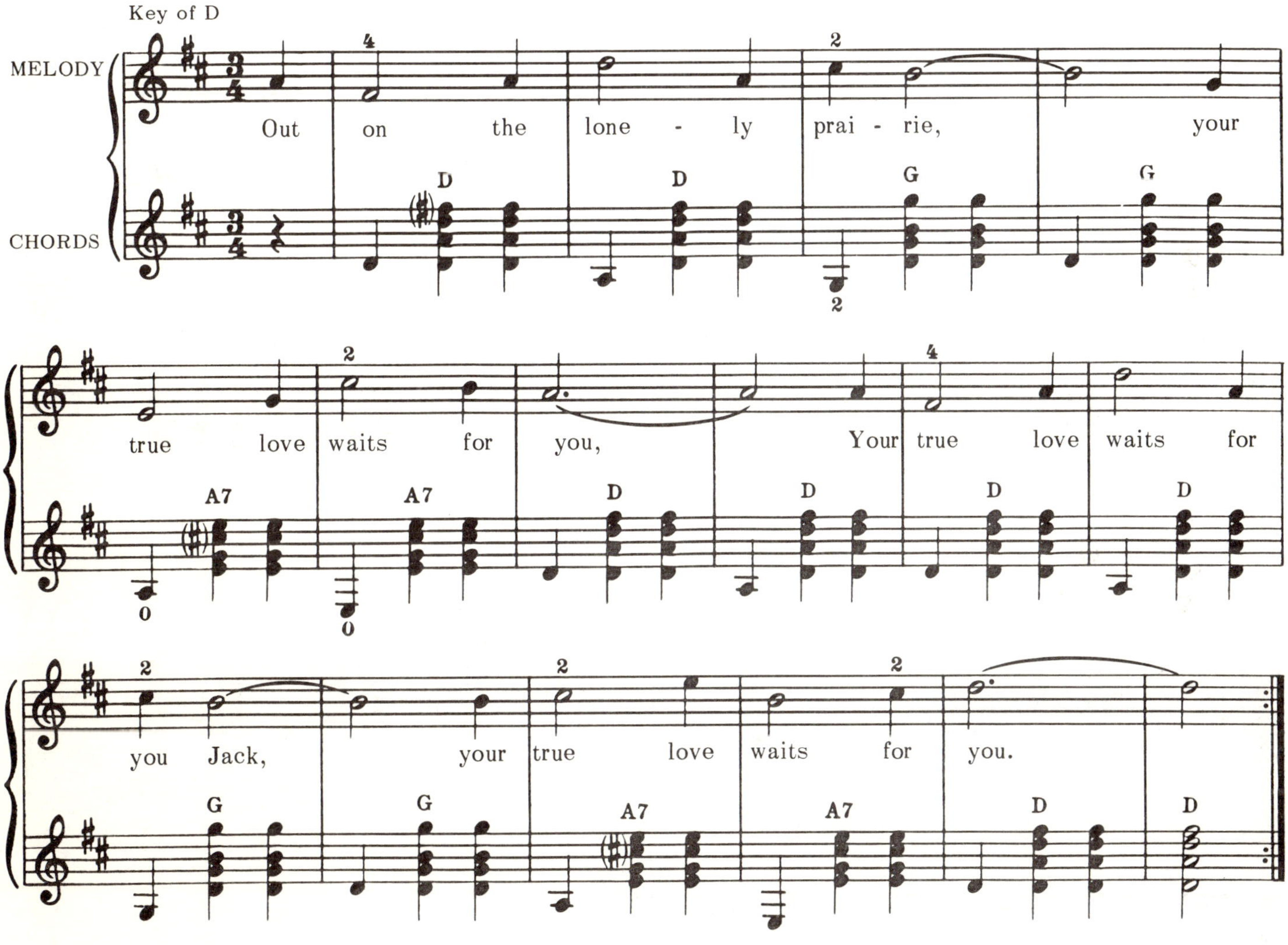

careless love

FOR TEACHER'S USE

old macdonald had a farm

you are the one near my heart

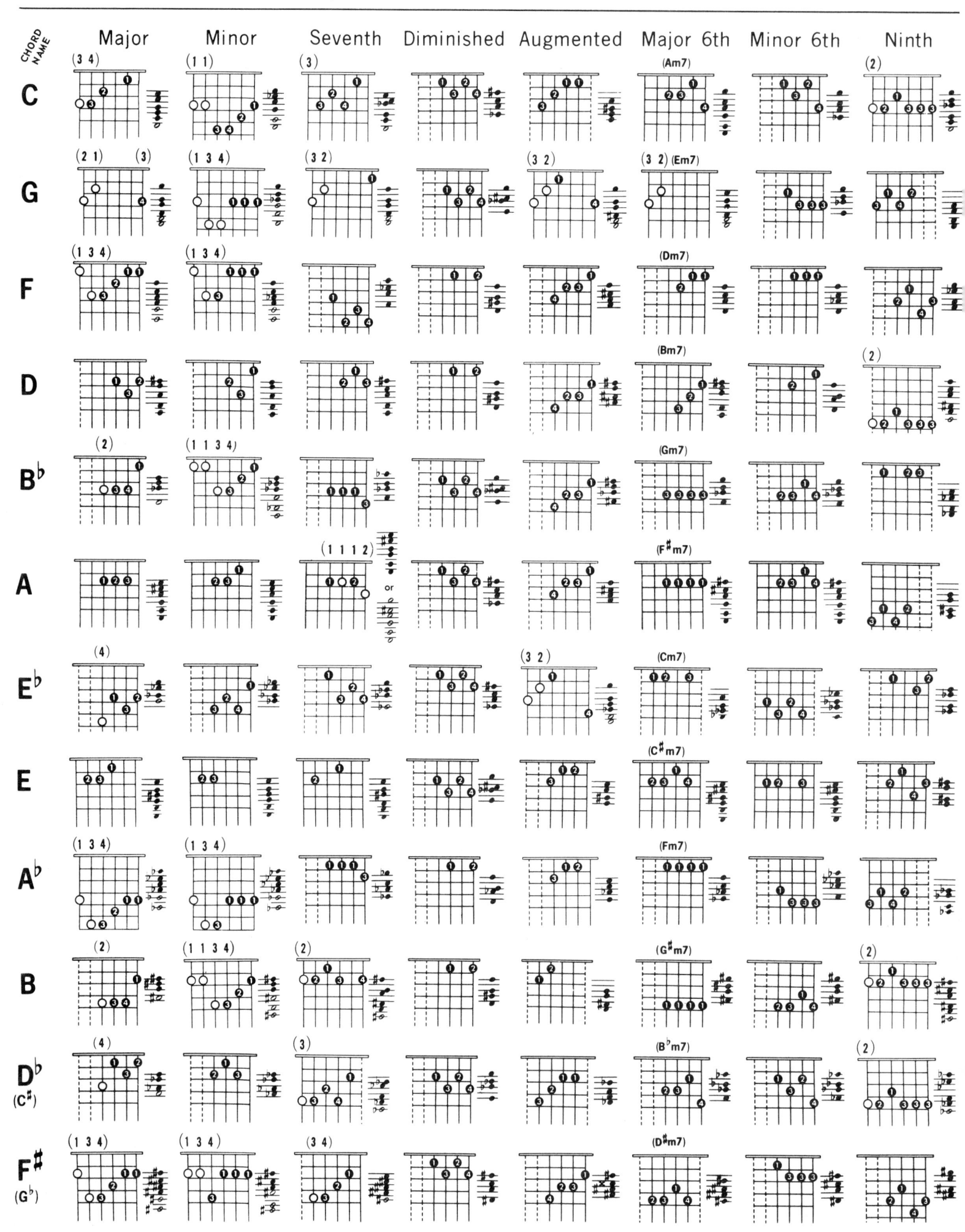